HAMLYN
WHO'S WHO
IN
GOLF

HAMLYN

WHO'S WHO

IN

GOLF

IAN MORRISON

HAMLYN

Photographic acknowledgements

Allsport, London 10, 21, 33, 38, 69, 73, 76, 90, 98, Jean-Marc Barey, Agence Vandystadt 124, Simon Bruty, 14, 15, 35, 36 right, 41, 51, 67, 74–5, 75, 100, 123, David Cannon title page, 9, 13, 17, 18, 19, 20, 22, 23, 24, 25, 27, 28, 29, 30–1, 32, 34, 37, 39, 43, 44, 45, 46–7, 48, 49, 52, 54 top and bottom, 55 top and bottom, 56, 57, 59, 60, 62, 63, 65, 66, 70, 71, 72, 79, 80, 83, 85, 87, 88, 89, 92, 93, 94, 95, 96, 97, 99, 101, 102, 103 left and right, 104, 105, 106 top and bottom, 108, 109, 110, 111, 112, 113, 114–15, 116, 118–19, 121, 122, Chris Cole 40, 125, Tony Duffy 42, Desmond Gross 8, Trevor Jones 77, Robert Martin 107, 120, Simon Miles 36 left, Mike Powell 6, 53, 58, 68, 78, 82, 117, 126, Steve Powell 11, 61, 86, Budd Symes 26; Colorsport, London 50, 64; Phil Sheldon, Barnet 84, 91, 127, Bob Thomas Sports Photography, Northampton 81.

Front cover: Allsport London Simon Bruty centre; David Cannon left, top right, bottom right.

Published by
The Hamlyn Publishing Group Limited
a division of The Octopus Group plc
Michelin House, 81 Fulham Road
London SW3 6RB
and distributed for them by
Octopus Distribution Services Limited
Rushden, Northamptonshire NN10 9RZ

First published in 1988

ISBN 0 600 55712 X

Printed by Mandarin Offset, Hong Kong

CONTENTS

Compiling a who's who in any sport is not a particularly difficult task because no matter which sport you select there are so many great names to write about.

Golf is certainly no different, as superstars like Jack Nicklaus, Arnold Palmer, Gary Player and Lee Trevino just keep going on and on, thus providing writers and journalists with ample material.

Including such men is an obvious starting point, but where does one draw the line? Who should be included? Who do you leave out? Now the job starts get-

Left: Severiano Ballesteros at the US PGA in 1987

Below: Laura Davies leading British golfer

ting tough. Having to choose 73 names from the hundreds of male and female golfers the world over, all of whom could rightly be included, makes the task of selection that much harder.

How does one decide a golfer's greatness? Is it based on his or her seasonal earnings which, after all, are a guideline to the current 'great' players. But, by that token, is Curtis Strange better than Seve Ballesteros? If you look at Strange's 1987 earnings of $925,941 compared to the £138,842 of the Spaniard then Strange is by far the better player . . . but is he? Don't forget prize money is bigger and there are more tournaments in the United States.

Do you look at all-time career earnings as a criterion? If so, Andy Bean's $2.5 million makes Arnold Palmer's $1.9 million look like chicken feed. But, with all respect to Andy Bean, how can anybody say his contribution to golf has been greater than Palmer's. Bean did his winning in the days of big prize money, which was partly due to Palmer's great contribution to the sport in the first place.

So where did I decide to draw a line?

All but three of the 73 entries are current players. Some like Arnold Palmer and Gary Player may be making their mark on the Seniors' Tour these days. But every player has been or is a champion. There are also some who have made their mark briefly, but could easily become a superstar of the future;

Bob Tway and Paul Azinger are two examples. Both men may never again have the same impact on the game as they did in 1986 and 1987 respectively, but the impact they had at the time was outstanding enough to warrant inclusion in this book.

How nice it would have been to have had dozens of Jack Nicklauses to write about, then the job would have been so much easier . . .

There were certain players that just *had* to be included. The top money-winners: Nicklaus, Tom Watson, Lee Trevino, Tom Kite, Ray Floyd etc were the obvious starting point, by virtue of their career winnings. Those men were then followed by winners of 'majors' such as Nick Faldo, Sandy Lyle, Larry Nelson and so on.

Then we had the problem of men like Johnny Miller and Fuzzy Zoeller. Both have had important wins and both have been winners of major championships, but neither are among 1988's elite of world golf. But whenever they turn out on a golf course they are guaranteed to attract a large audience. Because of that pulling power they cannot be omitted. Jerry Pate, John Mahaffey and Andy Bean all fall into that crowd-pulling category. For that reason they have entries in the book.

The aforementioned categories made up more than half the entries. But thereafter the problems really started. It was only fair to give the women a mention because the US LPGA Tour is expanding at a great rate and attracts huge amounts of sponsorship. Betsy King, JoAnne Carner, Jan Stephenson and Laura Davies could not be ignored, they have all made an impact on the game and are still doing so. After all it is a who's who in golf, not just a who's who of men's golf. How could Laura Davies be left out; she did as much to arouse interest in British golf in 1987, thanks to her victory in the US Open, as Nick Faldo did in the British Open, or her male counterparts did in winning the Ryder Cup.

Mention of the Ryder Cup brings us on to another category of entrants. All members of both teams that contested the 1987 match at Ohio are included. It was such an historic occasion that it would have been inappropriate to leave anybody out. Mind you, most of the players in the match would have justified an entry anyway.

We were finally left with the problem of finding the last batch of entrants.

To give the book a truly international flavour we looked at each of the golfing nations and felt it right to give their own heroes a mention. Tommy Nakajima and Isao Aoki have been outstanding in Japan and, while they have been impressive in both Europe and America, they have never had the breakthrough they deserve. But in their home country they have been two of the biggest money-winners the game has known. The same applies to Australia with Greg Norman, David Graham and Rodger Davis all of whom have been responsible for making their country a force to be reckoned with in world golf and consequently deserve an entry.

Finally, the game of golf does not end with the players. How can a who's who in golf be written without mention of Peter Alliss, one of the finest authorities on the game in Britain and the voice of golf for BBC Television. His right-hand man behind the microphone, entrepreneur Mark McCormack cannot be omitted either. His contribution to the sport's great growth in the 1960s must never go unnoticed. And finally how could the name of Tony Jacklin be left out of this book? As a player Tony's victories in the British and US Opens were the driving force for many youngsters. Now as the skilful captain of the European Ryder Cup team he has helped generate a new enthusiasm among golfers in Europe. It would have been an insult to Jacklin to have left him out.

There is a group of players who will always fall into the 'superstar' category and will always be the centre of attraction. There are others, however, who may have been top money-winners in 1987, but may never be heard of in 1988. On the other hand players will emerge in 1988 who were not much in evidence in 1987. It is inevitable because golf is such an unpredictable game. Those players will be included in future editions of this book.

Ian Morrison
April 1988

AMY ALCOTT

Born: 22 February 1956, Kansas City, Missouri, USA

Height: 5 ft 6 in (1.68 m)

Weight: 129 lb (58.5 kg)

Turned professional: 1975

First US LPGA Tour win: 1975 Orange Blossom Classic

Since turning professional and joining the US LPGA Tour in 1975 Amy Alcott has developed into one of the most consistent money-winners on the Tour and in 13 years never finished lower than 15th on the money-list. She started the 1987 season with 26 wins to her credit and career winnings of $1,800,000, third in the all-time list behind those two greats, Pat Bradley and JoAnne Carner.

Amy was the 1973 US Junior champion at 17 and five weeks after turning professional in 1975 won her first Tour event, the Orange Blossom Classic. She won a then record $26,798 by a first-year professional to take the Rookie of the Year title.

An extremely hard worker, Amy's only teacher was Walter Keller. She is constantly practising as she strives to improve her already efficient game. Her desire to win is the envy of many of her peers, and her competitive instincts are likened to those of a killer whale.

Despite her many Tour wins Amy has won the Women's US Open only once, but the way she won it you would have thought she was on a practice round. She led all the way to win by nine shots from Hollis Stacy and created an Open record with a four-round total 280, beating Jerilyn Britz's record of 284 set 12 months earlier. She tied the lead after the first round at the

Richland Country Club, Nashville, before winning with a 4-under par record on her way to collecting a $20,000 cheque, the first in US Women's Open history.

Amy had a chance of her second Open in 1984 when she needed a par-4 on the difficult 18th at Salem to force a play-off with Stacy. She double-bogeyed with a six and lost out.

Away from the golf course

Amy serves on the American President's Campaign Council Against Drug Abuse and also devotes a lot of her time to the Multiple Sclerosis Society. She runs her own golf tournament every autumn in Los Angeles for the benefit of the Multiple Sclerosis Society.

Amy Alcott gave up her chance to go to college in order to join the LPGA Tour at the age of 18. She has proved that decision to be right, and her continued hard work will keep her at the top of women's golf for many years. She has also recently written a book with Charles Shulz to help younger players.

'I used to think pressure was standing over a 4-foot [1.2-metre] putt, knowing I had to make it. Now I know that real pressure is 65 people waiting for their food with only 30 minutes left of their lunch break!'

Comparing the demands of golf and those of her spare-time job as a fast-food cook at the Butterfly bakery in Los Angeles

One of the biggest money-winners in women's golf, Amy Alcott

PETER ALLISS

Born: 28 February 1931, Berlin, Germany

Turned professional: 1946

First major European win: 1954 Daks Tournament

A brilliant striker of the ball, Peter Alliss' big failing was his lack of consistency with the putter. If that part of his game had not let him down so often he would have been one of the great British players in the early post Second World War years.

His father Percy was a professional and Peter took to the game at an early age, turning professional in 1946 when only 15, and shortly after becoming an England Boys' international. He played in his first British Open at 16 but over the next 20 years his best finish in the tournament he would dearly love to have won was joint eighth in 1954, 1961 and 1962.

Ryder Cup nightmare

In the mid-1950s however, Alliss did establish himself as one of the top players in Europe, winning the Open championships of Spain (twice), Portugal and Italy. After coming out of the RAF Peter gained his first Ryder Cup selection in 1953 but his debut was not one for the Alliss scrapbook – he required a chip and three putts from the edge of the green against Jim Turnesa. He lost his match by one hole and the United States won the trophy by just one match.

Nevertheless, the man with the perfect swing was selected again and between 1953 and 1969 he played in eight matches. Father Percy was also a Ryder Cup player.

Peter moved from Parkstone, Dorset, to Yorkshire's Moor Allerton course in 1970 to take up the professional's post and his reputation as one of the game's leading tutors was increasingly acknowledged, and his many books on golf are read by thousands of students of the game each year. His vast experience and knowledge took him behind the microphone of the BBC where he succeeded the great Henry Longhurst as the 'voice of British golf'.

The much respected talents of Peter Alliss have been recognized in many quarters, particularly by the PGA which elected him their captain for the second time in 1986, 24 years after first doing so.

The voice of British golf, Peter Alliss. A very good golfer in the mid-1950s, Peter is acknowledged as one of golf's leading authorities as a teacher and broadcaster

LEADING TOURNAMENT WINS

1956
Spanish Open

1957
British PGA Championship

1958
Italian Open
Spanish Open
Portuguese Open

1962
British PGA Championship

1965
British PGA Championship

ISAO AOKI

Born: 31 August 1942, Abiko, Japan	
Height: 6 ft (1.83 m)	
Weight: 168 lb (76.2 kg)	
Turned professional: 1964	
First Japanese Tour win: 1971 Kanto PGA Championship	

After 14 years as a professional, culminating in being the top money-winner in Japan in 1978 and 1979, Isao Aoki started venturing away from his home country in the late 1970s. He finished joint seventh in the 1978 British Open at St Andrews, the best placing ever by a Japanese golfer, and at the end of the season he won the prestigious World Match-Play title at Wentworth by beating New Zealand's Simon Owen 3 & 2. He reached the final again the following year but lost to American Bill Rogers by one hole, but Aoki went home as the owner of a £55,000 flat following his hole-in-one at the second hole during his match with David Graham.

The success story continued in 1980 when he finished second in the US Open at the Baltusrol course in New Jersey, the highest placing ever in one of the world's four major competitons by a Japanese golfer. He was paired with Jack Nicklaus in all four rounds and Aoki shot three opening rounds of 68 for a share of the lead with Nicklaus. Only a 68 by the 'Golden Bear' to Aoki's 70 in the final round prevented him being the first male Oriental winner of a major championship. The following month the British fans were treated to a championship-equalling 63 by Aoki in the third round of the British Open at Muirfield in Scotland.

Taking on the Americans

Isao has won more than 50 tournaments in Japan and after his success at Baltusrol he decided to test his skills against the best Americans and he joined the US Tour in 1981.

> ### LEADING TOURNAMENT WINS
>
> **1978**
> World Match-Play Championship
>
> **1983**
> Hawaiian Open
> Panasonic European Open

Two poor opening years saw him win no more than $46,000 in a season but in 1983 the second great period in the golf life of Isao Aoki unfolded.

In the Hawaiian Open he trailed Jack Renner by one shot going into the par-five 72nd hole. A birdie would have put him in a play-off but his third shot from 128 yards went in the hole for an eagle three and he became the first Japanese golfer to win on the US Tour. He ended the season with nearly $150,000 and on his way home he stopped off in England to contest the European Open at Sunningdale, Berkshire. He added to this great year with a win over Carl Mason, Nick Faldo and Seve Ballesteros.

> 'This is the greatest thrill of my career. Nothing like this has happened to me before.'
>
> *After winning the Hawaiian Open*

Early days

Aoki was introduced to golf as a caddie at the Abiko Golf Club and because he was the tallest of the caddies he was nicknamed the Tower after the Tokyo Tower. He would practise whenever he could, often before members arrived at the course, or when they had all finished playing. He turned professional in 1964 but had to wait seven years for his first win, the 1971 Kanto PGA. Two years later he won the first of five Japanese PGA titles and was the top money-winner for the first time in 1976. He has since won that title four more times. Most of his golf is played in Japan these days, but whenever he ventures out, to Britain or the United States, he is a welcome visitor.

A magic moment . . . Isao Aoki kissing the ball that gave him a hole-in-one during the 1983 World Match-Play Championship at Wentworth

STYLE POINTS

Has a very wristy and unorthodox swing and when he putts the toe of the putter is in the air. Defies all the teachings about the full turn of the shoulders.

PAUL AZINGER

Born: 6 January 1960, Holyoke, Massachusetts, USA	
Height: 6 ft 2 in (1.88 m)	
Weight: 170 lb (77.1 kg)	
Turned professional: 1981	
First US Tour win: 1987 Phoenix Open	

Another Lema?

When Paul Azinger shot to the top of the leader board at the end of the second day of the 1987 British Open at Muirfield in Scotland people were comparing him with Tony Lema. (When Lema càme to Britain for the first time in 1964 there were many who said the flamboyant American would never be able to master the St Andrews course. They were wrong. He did, and furthermore he won the British Open by five shots from Jack Nicklaus.) The tall Azinger, with a strong resemblance to fellow professional Bill Rogers, had shot a second successive 68 to lead the field by one shot in his first-ever tournament on British soil.

Built like a bean-pole, and known as Zinger or the Gee Whizz Kid in the USA, he came to Muirfield as the leading money-winner on the US Tour, and he certainly showed why. He maintained his lead going into the final day and with half the final round behind him he led Britain's Nick Faldo by three shots. Another Lema-like fairytale was being prepared for the world's journalists. But it didn't turn out as expected.

Nerves affected the 27-year-old as he made mistake after mistake over the final nine holes. His most crucial error came at the 17th when he took a wooden club off the tee when an iron would have sufficed. He found a bunker, could only play out safe, and bogeyed with a six.

The two leaders were level and Faldo had completed his round. Azinger needed a par-4 at the 18th to force a play-off. He found sand again and had a 20-footer (6-metre) to stay in the game. It was no good, he missed and gave Britain her second champion in three years.

One only had to look at Azinger's face to share his anguish. He knew he had not *lost* the British Open, he knew he had *thrown it away*.

A young beginner

Paul Azinger first played golf when he was five. His parents both played the game and used to take him along with them. He had the alternative of hanging around being bored or picking up a club and trying to copy them. He started playing seriously at high school but cut down on his practice because he enjoyed working at his father's marina. When he went to college he decided to concentrate more on his golf and was coached by Jim Suttie, who recognized Azinger's potential and introduced him to John Redman.

It was Redman who took him to the level he's at now. Within a year of working with Redman his average score was down from 79 to 72. He did enough to get his Tour card via the qualifying school, but was so in awe of the big names on the Tour that he could hardly play his own game. He qualified from the school at the end of 1983 and in

his first season on Tour finished 144th with earnings of $27,000. That autumn he went back to the school and in 1985 he jumped 51 places on the money-list and boosted his earning by $54,000.

He finished runner-up in two events in 1986, notably the Hawaiian Open where he finished second to Corey Pavin, and ended the season 29th on the money-list.

A memorable year

It was 1987 which established him as a top player. He won the fourth event of the season, the Phoenix Open, and then added the Las Vegas Invitational and Greater Hartford Open as he climbed to the top of the money-winning list where he stayed most of the year until being overtaken by Curtis Strange at the end of the season. Even so he won a staggering $822,550.

His progress up the golf ladder to being a top earner in the USA has been in his own words: 'Amazing really'. Azinger is one of the best short-game golfers in the world and his bunker play is outstanding. To create such an impact in the USA as he did in 1987 sums up his true qualities. He showed signs of losing his nerve at Muirfield but, after all, it was his first visit to the British links. That experience will hold him in good stead for the future, which looks long and healthy.

'Don't worry about me, it'll make me a better player for next year.'

After losing the 1987 British Open

STYLE POINTS

Plays well out of traps and is very consistent in getting the ball close to the pin.

The power of the new golden boy of American golf, Paul Azinger. After a season-long battle with Curtis Strange in 1987, and with three US Tour wins behind him, Azinger conceded the top money spot to Strange. At Muirfield Azinger came close to winning the British Open at the first attempt

HUGH BAIOCCHI

Born: 17 August 1946, Johannesburg, South Africa	
Height: 6 ft (1.83 m)	
Weight: 170 lb (77.1 kg)	
Turned professional: 1971	
First European Tour win: 1973 Swiss Open	

Two events which dramatically changed Hugh Baiocchi's career happened within a week of each other in 1983. Having been banned from playing in the 1983 Scandinavian Enterprise Open because he was South African, Baiocchi could spend more time that week with his wife and daughter Lauren. The following week Baiocchi went to the Belfry course in Sutton Coldfield in England for the State Express Classic.

South Africa's Hugh Baiocchi, a regular winner in Europe since turning professional in 1971

Out of the mouths . . .
His 10-year-old daughter Lauren had enjoyed having her father spend so much time with her that when he went off to play at the Belfry she said to him: 'When you've won, we'll do this, and then we'll do that'. Baiocchi noticed it wasn't 'If you win' but 'When you win' which gave him great confidence after a couple of years' poor results. He won a three-way play-off with Eamonn Darcy and Mike Sullivan.

Had it not been for that uplift and the subsequent win which brought him out of the worst slump of his career, Baiocchi could well have left the Tour because he was seriously thinking of quitting and taking a job as a club professional back home in South Africa, and thus offering his family some security.

He had been in the top 30 on the Order of Merit every year since he joined the Tour in 1972, including second to Ballesteros in 1977. But in 1981 and 1982 he was 31st and 39th respectively. Since that win at the Belfry, however, he has continued to give his family financial security as he has been among the top winners even though another Tour win has not been forthcoming.

Tall, with an elegant swing, Hugh won the Brazilian and South African amateur titles before turning professional in 1971. He has since won many tournaments in Europe and his native South Africa. He followed up international honours from his amateur days by representing South Africa in the World Cup, and was, along with Gary Player, in the team that finished second to the American pair of Nicklaus and Miller at Marbella in 1973. In 1978 he was honoured with the captaincy of the South African PGA.

SEVERIANO BALLESTEROS

Born: 9 April 1957, Pedrena, Spain	
Height: 6 ft (1.83 m)	
Weight: 177 lb (80.3 kg)	
Turned professional: 1974	
First European Tour win: 1976 Dutch Open	

Golf runs in the Ballesteros family: Uncle Ramon Sota was a professional and finished sixth in the 1965 US Masters behind Jack Nicklaus and Seve's three brothers, Manuel, Baldomero and Vicente all played golf to a high standard. His father, also Baldomero, was not a golfer but a long-distance runner and a rower, winning several national titles with the Pedrena Rowing squad.

Good training ground
The family's 19th-century farmhouse overlooked the Real Club de Golf de Pedrena. The course, hilly and open to the elements from the imposing Santander Bay, was a tough, but good training ground for the four golf-playing Ballesteros brothers.

Seve first picked up a golf club at the age of seven but could not afford golf balls. Pebbles from the local beach were used instead. He started caddying when he was eight. Two years later he played in his first tournament and came fifth after shooting a nine-hole total of 51. He won his first tournament, the local caddie championship, when he was 12, and shot a remarkable 79.

Scratch golfer at 12
At such an early age Seve was considered a scratch golfer and,

after watching her four sons take up golf, his mother Carmen pronounced that Seve would become a world beater one day, the first of many people to predict a successful career for the likable Spaniard.

Seve's talent was confirmed when he won the 1973 caddies' title with a round of 65. The following year, at 16, he became Spain's youngest ever professional golfer.

The world takes notice
His first year on the European Tour saw him collect £2,915 in prize money and finish 118th in the Order of Merit. A year later he jumped to 26th and in 1976, following his first Tour successes in the Dutch Open and Lancôme Trophy, he was top.

Ballesteros certainly arrived in 1976, and it was not only the European public which had the chance to see the birth of a new golfing superstar: the whole golfing

What a great moment! Ryder Cup match-winner Severiano Ballesteros (right) with his European team captain Tony Jacklin

world was made aware of the young Spaniard after his performance in the Open at the Royal Birkdale course in Merseyside.

He had little or no regard for the great names challenging him at the top of the leader board as he blasted two opening rounds each of 69. It was only on the final day when he shot a 74 that he fell away and let in Johnny Miller. Ballesteros tied in second place with Jack Nicklaus but he had done enough to alert the golfing world to his talents.

'He was like a Ferrari and made us look like Chevrolets.'

Tom Kite's description of Ballesteros after the 1980 US Masters

---

The first major

He headed the European money-list again in 1977 and 1978 and then the inevitable first win in one of the world's four major tournaments came his way. The 1979 British Open was at Lytham in Lancashire and Ballesteros shot a course record 65 in the second round. In the final two rounds he shot 75 and 70 to hold on to win by three shots from Jack Nicklaus and Ben Crenshaw. In those final 36 holes Ballesteros struggled to hit the fairways with his driver. That gave the public a chance to see another side of his game, his great ability to recover from any situation – car parks, rough – you name it, he had a shot for it!

Another Palmer?

Ballesteros maintained his consistent form in 1980 and took the US Masters at Augusta, Georgia. He celebrated his 23rd birthday on the first day of the tournament. Four days later he was given the best belated birthday present he could have wished for, the Masters coveted green jacket. Seve had already made his breakthrough on the tough US circuit by winning the Greater Greensboro Open in 1978 and the American people relished the rare talent of the youngster, and comparisons were quickly made between him and their own hero, Arnold Palmer.

The win at Augusta opened the door for successes across the Atlantic and three years later Seve was again to don the famous green jacket after winning his second Masters title. His victory, by four shots, was just as resounding as that of 1980.

He won his second British Open at St Andrews in 1984 when he beat his great rival Bernhard Langer, and Tom Watson, by two shots. He had joined the US Tour at the beginning of that year, but he remained on it for only two years. The US Tour rules required a player to compete in 15 tournaments to retain his card. Ballesteros didn't comply in 1985 and Tour Commissioner Deane Beman implemented the rule, which led to a lot of ill-feeling between the two men. The US Tour's loss was Europe's gain because Ballesteros returned to the European Tour and broke a host of records.

The top match-play golfer

Since 1981 Seve Ballesteros has had an impressive record in the Suntory World Match-Play Championship at Wentworth. This is his season-by-season record:

1981	Final	Beat Ben Crenshaw	1 hole
1982	Final	Beat Sandy Lyle	37th hole
1983	Semi-final	Lost to Greg Norman	1 hole
1984	Final	Beat Bernhard Langer	2 & 1
1985	Final	Beat Bernhard Langer	6 & 5
1986	2nd round	Lost to Rodger Davis	7 & 6
1987	Semi-final	Lost to Ian Woosnam	1 hole

Records galore . . . but still a bad year!

In 1986 he took his European career earnings past the £1 million mark, and his season's earnings were a record £240,000. His six wins were just one short of the 33-year-old record and his stroke average was an amazing 68.95.

Since becoming a professional in 1974 Spain's Seve Ballesteros has risen to the top of the golfing world. Not only has he dominated European golf but he has shown the Americans he can take them on and beat them on their home ground

Despite all those records, Seve still regarded 1986 as a bad year.

Firstly, his father died just a couple of weeks before the US Masters and then, in the tournament itself, he threw away a great chance to win his third Masters. As he stood on the tee at the 15th on the final day he was three up on Jack Nicklaus. His second shot, a number 4 iron, and probably the worst shot of his life, found water. He bogeyed the hole, and the next one; Nicklaus picked up birdies and suddenly his lead had gone, and the chance of a third Masters.

Although surrendering his European crown to Ian Woosnam in 1987 Seve had the honour of holing the winning putt in the Ryder Cup

> **'In the United States I'm lucky. In Europe I'm good.'**
>
> *On how the press on both sides of the Atlantic used to view him*

at Muirfield Village, having been a great inspiration to the team in both 1985 and 1987.

STYLE POINTS

Stands far behind the ball when putting. Uses his knees to help play the shot when chipping.

Ballesteros seems to be in a bit of trouble again . . . but that doesn't bother him, he is the master of the recovery shot . . .

ANDY BEAN

Born:	13 March 1953, Lafayette, Georgia, USA
Height:	6 ft 4 in (1.93 m)
Weight:	225 lb (102 kg)
Turned professional:	1975
First US Tour win:	1977 Doral-Eastern Open

At 6 ft 4 in (1.93 m) Andy Bean is one of the tallest men on the US· circuit. Not surprisingly he is also one of the longest hitters on the Tour as well

Andy Bean is a man who once wrestled with an alligator. He also bit a golf ball in half in anger on another occasion. But underneath that exterior is one of the US Tour's nice guys with a heart to match his size. He is also one of the game's biggest hitters. His large hands generate so much power, but on the delicateness of the putting surface they serve him just as well.

The money rolls in

A professional since 1975, he took less than ten years to amass winnings of $2 million on the US Tour. That statistic alone gives an indication to the level of consistency of Andy Bean.

In the four years from 1977 he finished 12th, 3rd, 7th and 4th in the money-list and had chalked up six Tour wins. He kept on winning, despite badly damaging a wrist in 1981. A fracture at the base of his left thumb kept him out of action for a large part of the season but he still managed to win $105,000. When he beat George Archer, who was trying for his first win in eight years, to win the Greater Greensboro Open in 1984 it was Andy's first win for nearly three years and, for the first time since his injury Bean once more felt comfortable on a golf course. The consistency in his game returned and he finished the season with a personal best $422,995 and was third in the money-list.

A year without a win in 1985 saw another mini-slump but two wins in 1986 put him back in the top five. He had won nothing in 1987 until retaining the end-of-season Kapalua International at Hawaii.

Dad owning a golf course helped!

Andy Bean has been luckier than most budding golfers – his father owned a golf course!

When the family moved from Georgia to Lakeland in Florida, his father, a keen golfer, bought a local golf course. It gave Andy, then aged 15, the chance to play golf whenever he wanted, and naturally his parents encouraged him totally.

Bean came through the US Tour qualifying school in the autumn of 1975, but won only $10,000 in his first season. The following year he won his first event, the Doral-Eastern Open, which he has won three times in his career. The victory was made even sweeter by the fact that he clinched it on 13 March – his 24th birthday.

Since then consistent has been one of the most widely used adjectives in describing Andy's game. He has never won a major competition although he finished second to Jack Nicklaus in the 1980 US PGA Championship at Oak Hill, New York, and was joint second to Tom Watson at Royal Birkdale in Merseyside in the 1983 Open. If he had not cut his tee-shot into the rough at Birkdale's 18th it could have been a different story.

STYLE POINTS

Packs a lot of power into his shot. Winds up before he starts his downswing. A long hitter.

LEADING TOURNAMENT WINS

1977
Doral-Eastern Open

1978
Kemper Open
Danny Thomas–Memphis Classic
Western Open

1979
Atlanta Classic

1980
Hawaiian Open

1981
Bay Hill Classic

1982
Doral-Eastern Open

1984
Greater Greensboro Open

1986
Doral-Eastern Open
Byron Nelson Classic
Kapalua International

1987
Kapalua International

PAT BRADLEY

Born: 24 March 1951, Westford, Massachusetts, USA

Height: 5 ft 6 in (1.68 m)

Weight: 126 lb (57.2 kg)

Turned professional: 1974

First US LPGA Tour win: 1976 Girl Talk Classic

At the end of the 1987 season Pat Bradley, with career winnings of over $2½ million, was the biggest money-winner in the history of women's golf.

Pat started playing golf at the age of 11 under the watchful eye of her father Richard although her formative years were under the guidance of instructor Gail Davis.

'It's been a year I'll never forget – Bradley is now the player people thought she would be. It's just taken me longer than I thought.'

Summing up her great year in 1986

She turned professional in 1974.

Pat won her first major tournament in 1981 when she was engaged in one of the best confrontations the world of women's golf has ever seen before going on to win the US Women's Open. At the La Grange Country Club in Illinois, Pat and Beth Daniel were level at the end of the sixth hole in the final round and for the next ten holes matched each other stroke for stroke. The sequence was broken at the 16th when Pat sank a monster 75-foot (23-metre) putt for a two at the par-3 and that was enough to give her victory. 'I was just trying to get close and the darn thing went in', she admitted. But it was enough to give her the title.

The Grand Slam

No matter what Pat Bradley achieves in the future, it is unlikely she will ever eclipse her great 1986 season.

She dominated the US Tour with five wins, including three of the majors, the Nabisco Dinah Shore, the LPGA Championships, and the du Maurier Classic, making her the first person to complete the women's Grand Slam. She also won a record $492,021, became the first woman to surpass career earnings of $2 million, and was, understandably, the Player of the Year.

Naturally, it was a hard act to follow and Pat slipped down the rankings in 1987.

Away from the golf course

When not playing golf Pat enjoys herself on the ski slopes. It is a pastime she loves and is very proficient at, and at one time she was a ski instructor. If she had not turned to golf she always had a second sport to fall back on.

Pat's greatest fans are her parents and whenever Pat wins a tournament they go through the ritual of ringing a bell on the back porch of their home, no matter what time of day or night it is!

Pat Bradley with the Nabisco Dinah Shore trophy, one of three women's majors she won in 1986

LEADING TOURNAMENT WINS

1980
Peter Jackson Classic

1981
US Women's Open

1985
du Maurier Classic

1986
US LPGA Championship
Nabisco Dinah Shore
du Maurier Classic

GORDON J. BRAND

Born: 6 August 1955, Cambridge, England	
Height: 5 ft 10 in (1.78 m)	
Weight: 175 lb (79.4 kg)	
Turned professional: 1976	
First major professional win: 1981 Ivory Coast Open	

A 'Senior' at 30?

Since the arrival of another Gordon Brand (no relative) on the European Tour in 1981 Gordon has had to change his name – twice. He became Gordon Brand Senior (as opposed to Junior) but more recently has called himself Gordon J. Brand – the senior tag did not do justice to this 32-year-old.

A professional since 1976 and a regular member of the European Tour, Gordon J. Brand was still waiting for his first Tour win at the end of the 1987 season. Despite his lack of success in Europe, however, he has proved himself the most outstanding player on the Safari Tour since the mid-1970s. In winning the 1987 Zimbabwe Open he won his fifth title and at the end of the 1987 campaign his total winnings on the Tour had reached a record £107,000 which was more than £17,000 better than second placed Bill Longmuir.

A former English amateur international, Gordon won his first big professional event with the Ivory Coast Open in 1981. He was also the winner of the Tooting Bec Cup for the lowest round in the 1981 British Open at St George's course at Sandwich in Kent, despite finishing 19th. His second-round 65 included a hole-in-one at the 16th.

Since 1983 Gordon has been a top 25 finisher on the Order of Merit four times and in 1983 was selected for the European Ryder Cup team to play at White Sulphur Springs in West Virginia. He played only in the final-day singles, and lost to Bob Gilder. His best season was in 1986 when he won £115,000 in Europe and finished fifth on the Order of Merit. Those winnings were swelled by £50,000 after finishing second to Greg Norman in the Open at Turnberry in Ayrshire, Scotland. Although five behind Norman his consistency gave him the outright second place despite such notable men as Bernhard Langer, Nick Faldo and Seve Ballesteros breathing down his neck.

Before taking up golf full time Gordon played cornet in a Yorkshire sauce works brass band. He also had ambitions to be a professional footballer but his love of golf soon overtook those ideas.

Gordon J. Brand during the 1987 Dunhill Cup. Howard Clark and Nick Faldo were his team-mates in beating Scotland to win the cup

LEADING TOURNAMENT WINS

1981
Ivory Coast Open

1983
Nigerian Open

1986
Nigerian Open
Ivory Coast Open

1987
Zimbabwe Open

GORDON BRAND, JNR

Born: 19 August 1958, Burnt Island, Fife, Scotland	
Height: 5 ft 8 in (1.73 m)	
Weight: 166 lb (75.3 kg)	
Turned professional: 1981	
First European Tour win: 1982 Coral Classic	

As an amateur Gordon Brand junior won the English Amateur Stroke-play title, British Youths' Open, Swedish Open, Scottish Open and Portuguese Open, as well as playing on the 1979 Walker Cup team. A fine pedigree indeed but often a good amateur record counts for nothing when making the transition to the professional game. Brand, however, followed on where he left off when he turned professional in 1981 after being overlooked for a second Walker Cup appearance.

Gordon won the PGA qualifying school at the end of 1981 and rehearsed for his debut pro year by spending the winter months in South Africa, where he finished second to Gary Player in the South African PGA Championship.

Rookie of the year

Given the Junior tag by the European PGA to distinguish him from the older Gordon Brand, he was the 1982 Rookie of the Year, won two tournaments, collected more than £40,000 in prize money and was seventh on the Order of Merit.

In his first professional European outing, the Tunisian Open, he finished third but two months later he opened his account by winning the Coral Classic at Royal Porthcawl in South Wales, three shots ahead of Greg Norman. In winning, Gordon became the first Rookie to win a European PGA event since Ronnie Shade won the Carrolls tournament in 1969. Before the season was over he collected another £15,000 for winning the Bob Hope British Classic at Moor Park, Hertfordshire, finishing three shots ahead of Mark James.

Decline and revival

Although born in Scotland Gordon was brought up in the Bristol area where his father was the professional at Knowle Golf Club. It was his father who noticed a fault in Gordon's address in 1983 which resulted in him going through his second season without a win and a dramatic slip down the Order of Merit to 34th. His father worked on Gordon's problem and in 1984 two more wins and prize money of nearly £63,000 saw him

back up to seventh place. Gordon's confidence returned and at the end of the year he helped Scotland to second place in the World Cup, and finished runner-up in the individual competition.

Gordon finished in the top ten on the Order of Merit in both 1985 and 1986 even though he was without a win. The end-of-season run in 1985, when he came third in the European Open and second in the Spanish Open, came too late for him to land a Ryder Cup place, but he had no such problems in 1987 when successive wins in the Dutch Open and Scandinavian Enterprise Open helped him towards £100,000 winnings for the second season running, but more important, guaranteed him a place on Tony Jacklin's winning team against the Americans at Muirfield Village in Ohio.

The white cap is frequently the easiest way to distinguish Gordon Brand Jnr from Gordon J. Brand. Their accents are quite different as well . . . Junior is Scottish!

KEN BROWN

Born: 9 January 1957, Harpenden, Hertfordshire, England

Height: 6 ft 2 in (1.88 m)

Weight: 155 lb (70.3 kg)

Turned professional: 1975

First European Tour win: 1978 Carrolls Irish Open

F ive years is a long time without a win in golf but between Ken Brown's first European PGA Tour win in 1978 and his second in 1983 he matured from being a brash hot-headed youngster into a top international competitor. He finally lost the 'one-wonder' tag in 1983 when he won the KLM Dutch Open, five years after his first Tour success, the Carrolls Irish Open.

In the interim years he had been in trouble with the golfing authorities because of his tantrums, and his behaviour during the 1979 Ryder Cup resulted in him being fined £1,000 and banned from international competition for 12 months.

Happily that sort of behaviour is a thing of the past for Ken Brown and he is now a respected member of the US Tour where he has been playing regularly since coming through the qualifying school in the autumn of 1983.

'I went to America for the sole purpose of becoming a better golfer. It would have been easy to sit on my bum making money and enjoying myself in Britain but the good America has done me is obvious.'

Youthful ambitions

Ken started playing golf at the age of 12. By the time he was 15 he knew he wanted to be a professional golfer. He won his first trophy as a 17-year-old when he played truant from school to win the Carris Trophy at Moor Park.

He turned professional at 18, working in a golf shop initially, and practising as often as he could. As a 20-year-old in 1977 he found himself in the Great Britain Ryder Cup team and the following year he won his first Tour event. He has since played on most Ryder Cup teams,

except in 1981, and was one of Tony Jacklin's three personal preferences for the 1987 team – an indication how he has progressed from those wild days of 1979.

Playing on the tough US Tour has had its benefits for Ken and he made a brief return to Britain in 1986 to pick up two cheques totalling £34,000 for finishing second

LEADING TOURNAMENT WINS

1978
Carrolls Irish Open

1983
KLM Dutch Open

1984
Glasgow Open

1985
London Standard *Four Stars Pro-Celebrity*

1987
Southern Open (US)

to Greg Norman in the European Open and then tying for second place behind Ian Woosnam in the Lawrence Batley Tournament Players' Championship. It was a reminder to people back home that, because he was playing in the States, he was not the forgotten man of British golf. Ken's confidence in his ability to win in the States was vindicated the week after the Ryder Cup success when he won the Southern Open.

Ken Brown always believed he was good enough to win on US soil. The breakthrough came in 1987 when he won the Southern Open

MARK CALCAVECCHIA

Born: 12 June 1960, Laurel, Nebraska, USA
Height: 6 ft (1.83 m)
Weight: 200 lb (90.7 kg)
Turned professional: 1981
First US Tour win: 1986 Southwest Golf Classic

As a teenager interested in golf, Mark Calcavecchia could not believe his good fortune when the family moved from Nebraska to Palm Beach in Florida when he was 13 years old. He could play golf all the year round and was so keen to play the game, he often played 72 holes in a day.

When he was 16 he won the Florida State Junior. He knew from then he was a winner at golf and dreamed of one day making the US Tour. That dream came true in 1981 when he qualified through the Tour school in the spring.

Life was tough for young Mark: he finished no higher than 134th on the money-list in his first four years and in 1985 lost his card after finishing 162nd. To make matters worse he did not get back on the Tour after failing to get through the Tour school.

'The greatest thing was playing golf on Christmas Day afternoon.'

On the family's move from Nebraska to Palm Beach

enough he could. That made Mark more determined to get back on the Tour. That determination paid off and he was back on the Tour in 1986. He won $13,500 for finishing eighth in his first competition of the year, the Doral-Eastern Open, and in the US Open at Shinnecock Hills on Long Island he attracted a

Texas. He finished 58th on the money-list and in 1987 realized his potential by adding a second win, the Honda Classic, and finishing tenth, earning more in the one season than in his other six years on the Tour put together. He also gained the great honour of being selected for the US Ryder Cup team, a far cry from Calcavecchia's disaster two years earlier when he lost his Tour status.

It was quite a year for Mark Calcavecchia in 1987. He finished 10th on the money list with over $500,000 – three times more than his previous best. He also gained his first Ryder Cup selection

Determination gets him back on the Tour

He spent a lot of time with his friend and fellow golfer Ken Green. Green told him that if he wanted to do something badly

lot of attention with a final-round 65 that equalled the course record.

Mark Calcavecchia's dream of Tour success eventually came true later in the year when he birdied three of the last five holes to win the Southwest Classic at Abilene in

STYLE POINTS

Gets long shots off the tee.

LEADING TOURNAMENT WINS

1986
Southwest Classic

1987
Honda Classic

JOSE-MARIA CANIZARES

Born: 18 February 1947, Madrid, Spain

Height: 5 ft 10 in (1.78 m)

Weight: 168 lb (76.2 kg)

Turned professional: 1967

First European Tour win: 1980 Avis-Jersey Open

One of the many fine players to come out of Spain in the 1970s – Jose-Maria Canizares, three times a Ryder Cup player

When Spain's Jose-Maria Canizares won the Bob Hope British Classic in 1983 it was not only his second win in the short-lived event but also ended a two-year run of seven second places on the European Tour without registering a win. He completed the last four holes birdie-eagle-birdie-birdie to defeat David Feherty by one shot. Despite being on the Tour since 1971 that was only his fourth win and he has not won a Tour event since then, although he won the 1984 Kenyan Open on the Safari Tour.

His first tour win was in 1980 when he won the Jersey Open and followed that by winning the inaugural Bob Hope British Classic at the RAC Club at Epsom, Surrey.

Canizares however, has not finished outside the top 25 on the Order of Merit since 1977, and has five times finished in the top ten. He also has a flair for low scoring and breaking records.

> **'It will now encourage every professional in Spain to bring more Spanish people into the game.'**
>
> *After he had helped Spain to a fourth World Cup win in 1984*

Canizares – record breaker

In the outward nine holes of the third round of the 1978 Swiss Open at Crans-sur-Sierre he set a Tour record, and equalled Mike Souchak's world record, with a score of 27. His 18-hole total included a record-equalling 11 birdies. Over the same course in 1986 he was one off the Tour record for 18 holes when he shot a 61 in the Ebel European Masters-Swiss Open.

He has proudly played for Spain six times in the World Cup and was a member of the winning team in 1982 with Manuel Pinero, a former schoolmate and fellow caddie in their younger days, and was one half of the 1984 winning team, with Jose Rivero. Canizares also took the individual title. He has always tried to encourage more Spanish youngsters to take up the game and emulate the feats of himself, Pinero, Garrido, Ballesteros and Rivero.

Canizares has played on three Ryder Cup teams, 1981, 1983 and 1985 but his drop down the Order of Merit in 1987 meant he missed out on further selection.

LEADING TOURNAMENT WINS

1980
Avis-Jersey Open
Bob Hope British Classic

1981
Italian Open

1982
World Cup team (with Manuel Pinero)

1983
Bob Hope British Classic

1984
Kenya Open
World Cup team (with Jose Rivero) and individual

JOANNE CARNER

Born: 4 April 1939, Kirkland, Washington, USA

Height: 5 ft 7 in (1.7 m)

Weight: 133 lb (60.3 kg)

Turned professional: 1970

First US LPGA Tour win: 1969 Burdine's Invitational (as an amateur)

JoAnne Carner during the 1987 Dinah Shore . . . no longer 'Big Momma' . . . more a case of 'Mini Momma'

Known as Big Momma, JoAnne Carner has been the darling of US crowds for more than 30 years. In 1987, at the age of 48, she came close to winning the US Women's Open for the third time, but lost a three-way play-off won by Britain's Laura Davies.

A win by JoAnne would have pushed her close to the legendary Bobby Jones' all-time US championship wins record of nine. She currently has seven to her credit including a post Second World War record five amateur titles.

> **'I did something by climbing over 113 golfers. The only trouble is there were 114 ahead of me.'**
>
> *Reference to the 1983 US Women's Open when she was lying 115th after a first-round 81. (She then shot 70, 72, 68 to tie second behind Jan Stephenson)*

Amateur champion at 18

As JoAnne Gunderson, and nick-named the Great Gundy, she reached the Amateur Championship final in 1956 at the age of 17 but lost to Canada's Marlene Stewart. A year later she became the second youngest winner of the title. From that day on JoAnne has known nothing but success. She appeared on four US Curtis Cup teams and won the 1969 Burdine's Invitational in Miami when still an amateur. No amateur has won on the US LPGA Tour since.

JoAnne turned professional late in life, and was nearly 31 when she joined the LPGA Tour. Since then, however, she has won more than 40 tournaments worth over $2 million, which makes her the second biggest money-winner in the Tour's history.

She was top money-winner in 1974, succeeding the great Kathy Whitworth, and in 1976 won her second Open. It was during that championship that she got her nickname when Sandra Palmer, who JoAnne beat in the play-off, called her Big Momma. The name has stuck ever since, but with the occasional modification.

Big Momma becomes Mini Momma

A great favorite with the fans and with her fellow professionals Jo-Anne was, in 1985, the tenth woman to be inducted into golf's Hall of Fame.

JoAnne has had to endure in-juries and illness in recent years. In 1979 a motorcycle accident put her out of action for most of the season. She bounced back to top the money-list in 1982 and 1983 but the following year she started feeling fatigued and inexplicable aches and pains appeared. Treatment and a strict diet put her back on the road to recovery. The diet resulted in a huge weight loss and her fans and the media re-christened her Medium Momma, later changed to Mini Momma.

Happily, the illness seems to be behind her, and at Plainfield, New Jersey, in the 1987 Open the 48-year-old JoAnne Carner showed why she is one of the greatest women golfers of all-time.

LEADING TOURNAMENT WINS

1957
US Women's Amateur

1960
US Women's Amateur

1962
US Women's Amateur

1966
US Women's Amateur

1968
US Women's Amateur

1971
US Women's Open

1976
US Women's Open

STYLE POINTS

A devastating bunker player and long driver.

TZE-CHUNG 'T.C.' CHEN

Born: 24 June 1958, Taipei, Taiwan

Height: 5 ft 10 in (1.78 m)

Weight: 145 lb (65.8 kg)

Turned professional: 1980

First major professional win: 1981 Sapporo (Japan) Open

Tze-Chung Chen, known affectionately as T.C., did not start playing golf until he was 17 but five years later he was a member of Taiwan's World Amateur Cup team, and finished second in the individual competition to America's Hal Sutton. He turned professional that year, 1980, and within seven years of first taking up the game he was playing among the world's top golfers on the US Tour.

He was introduced to golf by his older brother Tze-Ming (known as T.M.), who finished joint third in the 1985 US PGA Championship. T.C. used to caddy for T.M. when he played the Asian Tour but it was not long before T.C. joined the Tour himself and in 1981 he won the Sapporo (Japan) Open.

The States next stop

An accurate, if not very long hitter, T.C. went to the USA in 1982 and qualified through the Tour school that autumn. He came close to victory in his first season when he tied with four other players in the Kemper Open but lost the five-way play-off to Fred Couples.

So near yet so far

Chen attracted a lot of worldwide attention in 1985 during the US Open at Oakland Hills, Michigan. He equalled the competitive course record with a 65 on the first day and was leader for the first three days. He went into the final round with a two-shot lead over Andy North. But then, disaster! Standing on the fifth tee he led North by four shots. Standing on the sixth tee they were all square. Chen took a quadruple bogey eight. He then bogeyed the next three holes. He finished with a 77 and a triple tie for second place behind North.

Chen has found the Tour tough, and struggled in his first four years, finishing no higher than 68th in his Rookie year. His patience was rewarded in 1987 when he beat Ben Crenshaw in a play-off to win his first event, the Los Angeles Open, and he took his earnings for the season past $250,000.

One of the top players from the Far East, and a popular member of the US Tour, Tze-Chung Chen, known as 'T.C.'

LEADING TOURNAMENT WIN

1987
Los Angeles Open

HOWARD CLARK

Born: 26 August 1954, Leeds, England
Height: 6 ft 1 in (1.85 m)
Weight: 190 lb (65.8 kg)
Turned professional: 1973
First European Tour win: 1978 Portuguese Open

Britain's Howard Clark has finished among the top ten in the Order of Merit for the four seasons beginning 1984 and was in the 1985 and 1987 winning Ryder Cup teams

Since 1971, when he won the British Boys' championship as a 17-year-old, Howard Clark has risen to become one of the top players on the European circuit. He has ten Tour wins to his credit but one of the most pleasing performances of his career was in the 1981 Ryder Cup when he had six birdies and an eagle to beat Tom Watson 4 & 3 at Walton Heath in Surrey, although the USA won the trophy.

Later the tall blond Yorkshireman was one of the heroes of the European sides that defeated the American Ryder Cup teams at the Belfry course in Sutton Coldfield near Birmingham in 1985 and for the first time on American soil, at Muirfield Village, Ohio, in 1987.

Early success
The Howard Clark success story started when he gained international honours as a Boy International at 15. He later played at Youths level and went on to win senior England International and Walker Cup honours.

'You'll soon be sitting on top of the world.'

Message inside a fortune cookie Howard received while having a Chinese meal in 1985. A couple of months later he was the individual champion in the World Cup

He turned professional in October 1973 and spent his early days under the watchful eye of master golfer Henry Cotton at his Penina course in Portugal. It was at Penina that Clark made the big breakthrough in 1978 with victory in the Portuguese Open. Another success, in the Madrid Open, elevated him to fifth place in the Order of Merit.

Although the lowest he finished over the next five seasons was 28th, he never enjoyed another Tour win. But since 1984 he has won eight times, has finished in the top ten every year, and has three times topped £100,000 in a season. He has been a member of the Ryder Cup team since 1977 and in 1985 was the World Cup individual winner in California. During these great years Howard has had to overcome a nagging back complaint, but happily it did not affect his game.

His return to form in 1984 followed his second marriage, in November 1983.

Snooker, soccer and . . . what?
A keen snooker player and soccer fan, when he can find time in between golf tournaments Howard can be seen sitting in the stand at Elland Road watching his local team, Leeds United. In his spare time he is a scripophilist, a collector of old stocks and share certificates.

Howard came to the professional game with an aggressive attitude and at times had difficulty controlling his emotions. He has grown out of that with maturity although he still has sufficient aggression to make him a winner.

LEADING TOURNAMENT WINS

1978
Portuguese Open
Madrid Open

1984
Madrid Open
Whyte & Mackay PGA

1985
Jersey Open
Glasgow Open

1986
Madrid Open
Spanish Open

1987
Moroccan Open
PLM Open

STYLE POINTS
Dynamic with the wedge and sand wedge.

BEN CRENSHAW

Born: 11 January 1952, Austin, Texas, USA
Height: 5 ft 9 in (1.75 m)
Weight: 170 lb (77.1 kg)
Turned professional: 1973
First US Tour win: 1973 San Antonio-Texas Open

Playing the first tournament on the US Tour is a moment any new professional remembers all his life. Winning the event, and then finishing second in your next outing is something that dreams are made of. But that is what happened to Ben Crenshaw in 1973.

To add further flavour to his inaugural win, it was the Texas Open at San Antonio – not far from Crenshaw's birthplace at Austin in Texas. Furthermore, his first ever round as a professional was a 65 and he led throughout to beat Orville Moody by two shots.

In his second event, the $500,000 World Open at Pinehurst in North Carolina, he finished second to Miller Barber.

Top amateur

That start to his career was not altogether unexpected because he left the amateur ranks with a tremendous record behind him. He won the NCAA Championship three years in succession for the University of Texas, even though he had to share the 1972 title with team-mate Tom Kite. He was also runner-up in the 1972 US Amateur Championship. A final-round 68 by Crenshaw in that year's World Amateur Team Championship helped the United States to victory over Australia.

Ben turned professional in 1973 and came through the qualifying school late that year with honours, winning by an incredible 12 strokes from runner-up Gil Morgan. His arrival on the US Tour was likened to that of Jack Nicklaus some 11 years earlier. His debut season was certainly comparable to the great man's.

Since then Crenshaw has won more than $2 million and 13 Tour events including the highlight of his career, the 1984 US Masters.

An elusive first major

This first major championship win took eleven years from his professional debut, though. Near misses included the 1976 US Masters

Two very proud parents, Mr and Mrs Crenshaw with son Ben after he had won his first major, the 1984 US Masters at Augusta

when he finished second to Ray Floyd despite rounds of 70, 70, 72, and 67. In 1978 and 1979 he was tied second place in the British Open and in 1979 he came closest to his first major when he was involved in a play-off with Australian David Graham in the US PGA Championship at Oakland Hills in Michigan but Graham won at the third extra hole, after staying alive with 18- and 10-foot (5.5 and 3-metre) putts at the first two extra holes. Crenshaw became

only the second man to break 70 in all four round, but it still wasn't good enough to win.

Crenshaw had by then established himself as one of the top money-winners in the United States and regularly finished in the top 20. He also gained a reputation for being the best putter on the Tour. Crenshaw also became very popular with fellow professionals and golf fans the world over, particularly in Britain.

He slumped to 83rd on the rank-

ings in 1982 but came back a year later with his best-ever season. He won the Byron Nelson Classic and a personal best $275,000. He came close, also, to that elusive major once more. This time it was at Augusta, Georgia, but he had to be content with a share of second place with his old school pal Tom Kite, four strokes behind Severiano Ballesteros. After coming so close so often, he finally got it right in Augusta in 1984 to beat Tom Watson by two shots and collect

There are few golfers more popular than Ben Crenshaw. Fans and fellow professionals alike respect him and during the 1987 British Open at Muirfield one of the biggest cheers up the final fairway on the last day was for Ben, even though he was out of contention

LEADING TOURNAMENT WINS

1973
San Antonio-Texas Open

1976
Bing Crosby National Pro-Am
Hawaiian Open
Ohio Kings Island Open

1977
Colonial National Invitation

1979
Phoenix Open
Walt Disney World Team Championship (with George Burns)

1980
Anheuser-Busch Classic

1983
Byron Nelson Classic

1984
US Masters

1986
Buick Open
Vantage Championship

1987
New Orleans Classic

the $108,000 first prize. All those near misses were forgotten as Ballesteros handed over the famous winner's green jacket to Crenshaw.

He led after the first day with a 67, and on a course that many said was not suited to his game. He fell four behind after the second round, and was two adrift going into the final round but a final 18-hole total of 68 gave him a four-round total 277 for 11-under par, and a two-shot win over Watson. 'Ben deserved it' was Watson's

Play-off record

At the start of the 1987 season Ben Crenshaw had been involved in five play-offs for US Tour events – and lost all five. This is how he fared.

1978	*Bing Crosby National Pro-Am*	*lost to Tom Watson*
1979	*Western Open*	*lost to Larry Nelson*
1979	*US PGA Championship*	*lost to David Graham*
1981	*Bing Crosby National Pro-Am*	*lost to John Cook*
1981	*Texas Open*	*lost to Bill Rogers*

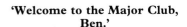

'Keep your eye on the club, not the ball.'

Some wag's comments to Crenshaw when, after he threw his club up in the air after hitting a poor shot during the 1986 US PGA Championship, Crenshaw didn't see where the club went, and must have forgotten Newton's law of gravity. The club came down and hit him on the head, necessitating several stitches to the wound!

generous remark in defeat; making reference to Crenshaw's years of coming so close to winning a big title.

Crenshaw, who once said he could not live without winning a major, simply described his win as 'A sweet, sweet thing', and added 'I don't think there ever will be anything sweeter for me'. The victory meant so much to him after years of near misses.

When he won the Masters in 1984 it was one of the most popular victories because there is not a player on the Tour that does not like Ben Crenshaw.

The mighty fallen . . . and re-arisen

People could not believe what happened to Ben Crenshaw the following season. He slumped to

'Welcome to the Major Club, Ben.'

Tom Watson to Ben Crenshaw after he won the 1984 US Masters

an all-time low of 149th on the Tour rankings and collected a mere $25,814 in prize money. However, it was discovered later in the season that he was suffering from a hyperactive thyroid. Once diagnosed, he was back to his competitive best in 1986 and finished eighth in the rankings with a personal best $388,000. He bettered that in 1987 when he finished third on the money-list behind Curtis Strange and Paul Azinger with winnings of $638,000. He also won his third Ryder Cup selection, having been picked in 1981 and 1983 when he was one of the USA's outstanding players in their one-point win over Europe. However, it was a different story in 1987. Playing Eamonn Darcy in the singles he broke his putter after hitting the ground in anger, after missing a putt at the sixth. He had to putt with a one-iron wedge after that, but only just lost on the 18th after a brave fight.

Crenshaw's hobby is collecting golf memorabilia and he always finds time to get to Britain whenever he can, in the hope of unearthing another rare book or piece of equipment to add to his already valuable collection.

Winning the Masters in 1984 ended a ten-year wait as a professional without a major for Ben Crenshaw

'I didn't want to have all night to think about that putt.'

On why he putted out for a birdie on the 13th during the final round of his US Masters win when lightning halted play and his partner had run for cover

EAMONN DARCY

Born: 7 August 1952, Delgany, Republic of Ireland

Height: 6 ft 1 in (1.85 m)

Weight: 182 lb (82.6 kg)

Turned professional: 1969

First European Tour win: 1976 Sumrie Better-Ball (with Christy O'Connor, Jnr)

Eamonn Darcy had a dramatic first five years on the European Tour. In his first year, 1971, he was 135th in the Order of Merit but his position improved to 122nd, 98th, 36th, 3rd and then

Since then he has been up and down but came back to eighth place in 1983 when he won his biggest prize at that time, the Spanish Open, which was added to the Kenyan Open he won in 1982.

stable. But he grew too big and had to turn to his second love, golf. He had been swinging a club since he was ten, and the switch to golf was an easy decision.

Since turning professional in 1969 Eamonn has won 11 tournaments worldwide, in countries as far apart as New Zealand, Australia, Kenya, Zambia, France, Spain, Belgium and Great Britain. He regularly competes on the Safari Tour and is one of the all-time top ten money-winners on the circuit. He has represented his country in the Hennessy Cognac Cup and World Cup, as well as being honoured with Ryder Cup selection.

After going without a win on the European Tour for four years, Darcy won the rain-interrupted Volvo Belgian Open at the Royal Waterloo Club in 1987 with a 54-hole total of 201 – one better than Nick Faldo, Ian Woosnam and fellow Irishman Ronan Rafferty. That win went a long way towards Eamonn filling the ninth place that guaranteed him Ryder Cup selection. And he did the team proud by beating the 'putter-less' Ben Crenshaw in the singles.

Darcy has won over £350,000 on the European Tour during his career which comfortably puts him in the top-20 of all time, highlighting how steadily he has played during his professional career.

There was no prouder member of the 1987 European Ryder Cup team than Eamonn Darcy, who holed a pressure putt for a singles victory

2nd in 1976 when only Seve Ballesteros won more money than him. That year Darcy won the Cacharel World Under-25 tournament in France.

From jockey to golfer

Darcy had set his heart on becoming a jockey because his County Wicklow home was close to top Irish trainer Paddy Sleator's

---

LEADING TOURNAMENT WINS

1982
Kenyan Open

1983
Benson & Hedges Spanish Open

1987
Volvo Belgian Open

——— STYLE POINTS ———

Unorthodox golf swing: he bends his left elbow and seems to have his right elbow too high but the position of the club head is spot on.

LAURA DAVIES

Born: 1964, Coventry, England	
Height: 5 ft 10 in (1.78 m)	
Weight: 161 lb (73 kg)	
Turned professional: 1985	
First professional win: 1985 Belgian Open	

Britan's top woman golfer Laura Davies

Sinking a 15-footer (4.6 metre) at the 14th and a 25-footer (7.6 metre) at the next hole set Britain's Laura Davies *en route* to her greatest victory, the 1987 US Women's Open and an accompanying cheque for £34,500, by far the biggest pay day of her career.

That day at Plainsfield, New Jersey, must have brought a smile to her face when she recalled how during the 1984 British Women's Open at Woburn in Bedfordshire club members from West Byfleet clubbed together and gave her £100 because she had no money.

In that short period, Laura Davies, the former supermarket check-out girl, has come a long way.

Games mad
At school the only thing she wanted to do was engage in sporting activities. She took five O-levels, but failed them all. Her teachers all said she would do better if she spent less time on the games field. A good hockey player, badminton player and athlete, she still joins the family in a tenpin bowling team in a local league when time permits.

She took up golf when she was 15, first at Guildford, then at Byfleet, but she has never had a proper golf lesson in her life. When things start going wrong she just goes out and practises until she cures it. She reduced her handicap from 26 to scratch in just 2½ years.

She tries to model her game on her two heroes, Bernhard Langer and Seve Ballesteros: her long game is styled on Langer's and her short game on Seve's.

Very shy in her amateur days, she would rather finish second than have to make the winner's speech. But that has changed as winning has become a way of life with Britain's top female golfer.

> **'If this girl were to play over here next year she'd be our leading money-winner.'**
>
> *Top American golfer Nancy Lopez after Laura's US Women's Open win in 1987*

The easy transition from amateur to professional
Laura was honoured with Curtis Cup selection in 1984, leaping ahead of some more seasoned players, but her selection was vindicated by her by beating the top American Anne Sander.

Laura turned professional in 1985 with £1,000 borrowed from her mother, and she won her first WPGA Tour event that year, the Belgian Open. She was top money-winner with £22,000 and the following year took her earnings to £37,500 after winning an unprecedented four Tour events in one year, including the British Women's Open at the Royal Birk-

dale course in Merseyside, to provide the first home win for eight years. Again she was top money-winner.

Golf's greatest prize
The pinnacle of her career was in winning the 1987 US Open to become only the fourth non-American to win the title, and the first British winner.

Caddied by her brother Tony at Plainsfield (regular caddie Tim Clark was lining up the St Mullion course in readiness for the British Open the following week), she displayed great cool and calm as she was pursued by such great names as JoAnne Carner and Betsy King. When sinking a difficult 4-foot (1.2-metre) putt at the 72nd hole to get into the three-way play-off she told herself 'It's all right if we miss, that way we'll be back in Britain in plenty of time for the Open'. She didn't miss and in the play-off beat Carner and Japan's Ayoko Okamoto to lift women's golf's top prize.

LEADING TOURNAMENT WINS

1986
British Ladies' Open

1987
US Women's Open

STYLE POINTS

Hits the ball a fair distance (260 yards–235 metres), and sometimes more, yet around the green she chips with such finesse. Grips the club far down the handle.

RODGER DAVIS

Born: 18 May 1951, Sydney, Australia	
Height: 5 ft 10 in (1.78 m)	
Weight: 170 lb (77.1 kg)	
Turned professional: 1974	
First professional win: 1977 McCallum's South Coast Open (Australia)	

There is no mistaking Rodger Davis. He's the natty dresser in the plus-fours with the personalized socks. But there is more to the genial Australian than his dress – he is rapidly emerging as one of the world's top golfers.

Davis showed great potential as a youngster and won many junior titles. He did not turn professional until he was 23, four years after marrying his biggest fan, wife Pam. He delayed turning professional to continue his accountancy studies at the Esso petroleum company.

A working professional at first, he became a tournament professional in 1977. He has been a regular on the European Tour since then and had his first Tour win in 1981 when he won the State Express Classic at the Belfry course near Birmingham. Before joining the European Tour he had enjoyed many successes in Australia, including beating Gary Player in a play-off to win the 1979 Victoria Open.

Years in the wilderness

His career and fortunes hit rock-bottom in 1981. His putting developed the dreaded 'yips' and it was so bad he left the game for a while. At the same time he lost a lot of money in a business venture and his mother died. Then in 1982 he met up with Graham Griffiths who agreed to sponsor Davis if he

'Get in my beauty' . . . the distinctive Rodger Davis on his way to winning the 1986 Whyte Mackay PGA Championship. It was his first European Tour win since 1981

LEADING TOURNAMENT WINS

1978
South Australian Open
West Australian Open

1979
Victoria Open

1981
State Express Classic

1985
Victoria Open

1986
Australian Open
New Zealand Open
Whyte & Mackay PGA

> **'It was tough, believe me, but looking back now it was great discipline and boy, was I fit!'**
>
> *On his early days as a working professional when he did a milk round as well as his duties at his club.*

wanted to get back into serious golf. It was thanks only to Griffiths that Davis was able to afford to return to the European Tour.

Things still did not go right, however. Davis was getting close to winning so many tournaments but was finishing second all too often. He was unimpressive in 1984 and finished 52nd on the money-list. Overweight as well, his game was beginning to sink to new lows.

Comeback

A fitness schedule was worked out for Rodger and he lost over 28 lb (13 kg). He reaped the benefit of it in 1986 when he enjoyed his best ever season.

The man with the long slow swing got his putting back together

and it was a 25-footer (7.6-metre) that forced a play-off with Des Smythe in the Whyte & Mackay PGA Championship at Wentworth in Surrey. Davis won the title with a 6 to Smythe's 7 at the third extra hole. He came close to winning again in the German Open but lost the play-off to Bernhard Langer and thus finished runner-up for the 31st time in his career.

At the end of the season, he swelled his already healthy bank balance by another £84,000 when, firstly, he finished fourth, losing to Jack Nicklaus, in the World Match-Play championship, again at Wentworth. He had earlier beaten defending champion Severiano Ballesteros by a massive 7 & 6.

He crowned a great year by gaining selection for Australia in the Dunhill Cup at St Andrews and helped his team retain the title by winning all four of his matches.

Rodger Davis's regular caddie is Brad Wright. Wright is a two-handicap golfer, and in his spare time runs a disco in Melbourne, Australia.

Davis was back on the European circuit in 1987 and continued to delight the fans with his pleasant personality and natty dress. He won a lot of friends during the 1987 British Open at Muirfield in Scotland. Having been the first-day leader he then slipped away slightly. However, he did something first-day leaders in the Open rarely do – come back into contention. It was only the consistent play of Britain's Nick Faldo that prevented a win for Davis who had to be content with a tie for second place with American Paul Azinger. If they had not been looking for a British win at Muirfield the Scottish fans at the Open would have been more than pleased to see Davis win the title.

Below left: Rodger Davis in familiar pose. Below: Davis with David Graham after Australia had won the Dunhill Cup at St Andrews in 1986

NICK FALDO

Born: 18 July 1957, Welwyn Garden City, Hertfordshire, England

Height: 6 ft 3 in (1.91 m)

Weight: 196 lb (88.9 kg)

Turned professional: 1976

First European Tour win: 1978 Colgate PGA Championship

'You must be mad' they told Nick Faldo when, at the end of the 1983 season, he decided to change his style. After all, he had just completed his most successful season by winning five European Tour events and finishing top of the Order of Merit with a record £140,761. So why the need to change?

New swing – new Faldo

He knew his swing would not last for ever and it was better to change before it was too late. He further knew his swing was not good enough to win him one of the majors. He slipped into obscurity and went three complete seasons without a win on the Tour. Many felt he would never come back but Faldo himself was completely dedicated to his new aim in life.

The man who helped him on the

'I want to find out where they made their mistakes.'

After winning the Open Faldo wanted to seek out Greg Norman and Tony Jacklin, past winners of the title, to find out what they did wrong after winning the title

road to a new career was Florida-based Dave Leadbetter. Towards the end of 1986 Leadbetter realized they were nearly there and all that was needed was a last bit of fine tuning. In 1987 Nick Faldo, 'born-again golfer', returned to winning on the European Tour.

England's top golfer Nick Faldo. He changed his style at the end of 1983 and it paid dividends as he returned to winning ways both in Britain and the United States

LEADING TOURNAMENT WINS

1978
Colgate PGA Championship

1980
Sun Alliance PGA Championship

1981
Sun Alliance PGA Championship

1984
Sea Pines Heritage Classic

1987
British Open

Furthermore his new swing won him the major he so desperately wanted.

An early win in the Spanish Open confirmed that Leadbetter and Faldo had got it right but the real test came in the British Open at Muirfield in Scotland a couple of months later. Faldo played four rounds of consistent golf, including a flawless last 18 holes made up of 18 pars to beat the unfortunate American Paul Azinger and Australia's Rodger Davis by one stroke. Faldo had added his name to the short list of post Second World War British winners of the title but more important he had come out of the wilderness and was no longer the forgotten man of British golf.

A steady putter all his career, it was his putter that won the title for Nick at Muirfield when he holed a 'missable' 4-footer (1.2-metre) to complete his round of 18 pars. Faldo had played the same shot hundreds of times as a youngster. 'This putt for the Open', he used to tell himself while on the practice greens. Now it was the real thing and he had all Britain waiting anxiously. Faldo didn't let them down.

Early days

The successful career of Nick Faldo stretches back to his days as a junior player. He was the British Youths' and English Amateur champion in 1975 at the age of 18. He was a professional the following year and by the time he was 20 was in the 1977 Ryder Cup team as the youngest ever British player, and to add to that he beat Tom Watson in the singles.

The star was well and truly born. He won the Skol Lager Tournament in 1977 and was that season's Rookie of the Year. His first win on the European Tour was the following year when he

Britain's second British Open winner in three years, Nick Faldo with the trophy after his 1987 win

won the PGA Championship which he won again in 1980 and 1981.

The US experience

From 1977 Faldo was constantly high among the top money-winners and was in the top ten six times. He gained valuable experience on the US Tour and became a regular member of the Tour in 1981. After playing 11 US events in 1983 he changed his plans and returned to Europe. His US experience showed as he won three consecutive events, starting with the French Open. He then went on to end the season with a total of five wins and top the Order of Merit. It

was then that the real professionalism of Nick Faldo showed through when he decided to change that swing.

He returned to the USA in 1984 and shot all four rounds in the 60s to win the Sea Pines Heritage Classic, the first Briton to win in the United States since Tony Jacklin in 1972. He was a member of the Ryder Cup teams, captained by Jacklin, that won in 1985 and 1987.

Since his great year in 1983 life has certainly changed for Nick Faldo. It is not only his swing that has changed but he has a new wife, Gill Bennett. Happiness, as well as a good golf swing, is the key to successful golf, and Nick Faldo will confirm that.

STYLE POINTS

Stays on the same plane throughout his swing, and keeps his left arm straight.

RAY FLOYD

Born: 4 September 1942, Fort Bragg, North Carolina, USA

Height: 6 ft 1 in (1.85 m)

Weight: 200 lb (90.7 kg)

Turned professional: 1961

First US Tour win: 1963 St Petersburg Open

What a year it was for the old-timers in 1986. First Jack Nicklaus became the oldest winner of the US Masters and then a couple of months later Ray Floyd, the man who keeps bouncing back, became the oldest winner of the US Open at the age of 43 years 9 months.

As a Rookie he won his first Tour event in 1963 when he captured the St Petersburg Open. He was only 20½ at the time and one of the youngest ever winners on the Tour. In between his two achievements Ray Floyd has compiled one of the most remarkable records in US golf.

Just when he is being written off back he comes with a vengeance . . . and with a few wins as well!

He steadily climbed up the ladder in his first six years on Tour but in 1969 set the game alight with wins in the Jacksonville Open, American Golf Classic and the US PGA Championship when he nearly threw away a five-shot lead but held on to win by one from Gary Player at Dayton, Ohio.

Written off once

Those successes saw him jump to eighth in the rankings but then a decline started and he went six years without a win and was being written off by the experts. But in 1976 he defied them all with wins in the US Masters and World Open and was joint runner-up in the US PGA Championship. He was seventh on the money-list and retained that placing a year later with two more Tour wins.

When he won the Masters he dominated the event and led from start to finish, setting 36 and 54 hole records and equalling Jack Nicklaus' 72-hole record for the championship with a 271. In his 72 holes he had a remarkable 21 birdies and one eagle. He won by eight shots from Ben Crenshaw

Ray Floyd in action during the 1986 Masters. Nicklaus went on to become the oldest winner of the title. A couple of months later Floyd became the oldest US Open winner at 43

LEADING TOURNAMENT WINS

1969
US PGA Championship

1976
US Masters

1981
Tournament Players' Championship

1982
US PGA Championship

1986
US Open

> **'I finally got me an Open. I don't think my career would have been complete without the Open.'**
>
> *After winning the 1986 US Open*
>
> **'I knew I was a pressure golfer when I was just 13 and competing against grown men for $100.'**

and was 11 ahead of third-placed Nicklaus. He was deprived of a notable double that year when Dave Stockton beat him by one stroke in the US PGA Championship at the Congressional course in Maryland.

Floyd remained as a top money-winner over the next seven seasons and in 1982 won his third major when he beat Lanny Wadkins into second place in the US PGA Championship at Southern Hills in Tulsa, Oklahoma. He led all the way after opening with a seven-under par 63 which he describes as 'The best round of golf of my life'. A double bogey at the 72nd hole cost him the PGA Championship record by one stroke.

Written off twice

A slump to 68th place on the money-list in 1984 had Floyd written off yet again. This time he was past 40 and there seemed little chance of him getting back into the big time. But age and statistics count for little in Floyd's vocabulary and he came back once more.

He won the 1985 Houston Open, his 19th Tour win, and was back among the top ten money-winners. A year later he notched up Tour win number 20 in dramatic style by winning the US Open at Shinnecock Hills on Long Island.

He came from behind on the final Sunday to win by one from

Chip Beck and Lanny Wadkins. The $115,000 cheque helped swell his season's earnings to over $380,000 and ninth on the money-list. Not content with winning the Open, Ray pocketed a further $90,000 for winning event number 21, the end-of-season Walt Disney World-Oldsmobile Classic.

Floyd was brought up in Fort Bragg, North Carolina and was the son of an army officer who is now the co-owner of the Cypress Lakes Golf Club in Fayetteville. Ray started playing golf at an early age but preferred baseball. It was after winning the National Jaycees Golf title in 1960, however, that he decided on a golf career and turned professional the following year. He

joined the Tour in 1963. His sister Marlene also plays professional golf and is a member of the US LPGA Tour.

Ray's career earnings from golf have been over $3,250,000 and he is the fourth biggest winner of all time behind Nicklaus, Watson and Kite. Although he has tended to let himself and his game slip at times, since the mid-1970s he has been a model professional and his dedication, determination and professionalism were seen at their best when he came through a quality field to win the US Open.

He went without a win in the 1987 season and he slipped more than 50 places down the rankings but he will surely be back.

Ray Floyd looking wet and cold . . . it must be in Britain! And so it was . . . during the 1987 Open at Muirfield, Scotland. Ray could only finish in a tie for 17th place

ANDERS FORSBRAND

Born:	1 April 1961, Karlstad, Sweden
Height:	6 ft 1 in (1.85 m)
Weight:	162 lb (73.5 kg)
Turned professional:	1981
First European Tour win:	1987 Ebel European Masters–Swiss Open

The brilliant but often inconsistent Swede Anders Forsband won his first European Tour event in 1987 but it came a week to late. If it had been seven days earlier he would have been an automatic choice for the Ryder Cup team and thus become the first Swede to play in the competition.

When he did win his first event, the Ebel European Masters–Swiss Open at Crans-sur-Sierre, there were no signs of that inconsistency as he won in majestic style with a 25-under par four-round total of 263. His final round of 62 included no fewer than 10 birdies. A year earlier Forsbrand came close to his inaugural Tour win in the same event but was beaten by the brilliant young Spaniard Jose-Maria Olazabal.

First Swede to win stroke-play event on Tour

In winning in Switzerland, Forsbrand became the first Swede to win a stroke-play event on the European Tour. Ove Sellberg and Mats Lanner had won match-play events previously.

Like the other Swedes, Forsbrand can hit the ball a long way when he connects properly. Otherwise he is a very talented golfer and the years should mature him and improve his accuracy.

Forsbrand spent some of his years learning golf on a Florida driving range where he worked for a while. Since turning professional in 1981, and joining the European Tour a year later, Anders' rise has been dramatic. In 1985 he was 34th on the money-list after collecting £15,500 for finishing just three shots behind Sandy Lyle in the Open at Royal St George's, Sandwich, in Kent. He turned in a quality performance that day and he continued his fine run in 1986 when he was eighth on the Order of Merit, and that was without registering a win. In 1987 however he won over £100,000 and now lives in the tax haven of Marbella.

Sweden's Anders Forsbrand made his big European breakthrough in 1987 by winning the Ebel European Masters-Swiss Open

LEADING TOURNAMENT WINS

1982
Swedish PGA Championship

1987
Ebel European Masters–Swiss Open

BERNARD GALLACHER

Born: 9 February 1949, Bathgate, Edinburgh, Scotland

Height: 5 ft 9 in (1.75 m)

Weight: 168 lb (76.2 kg)

Turned professional: 1967

First European Tour win: 1969 Schweppes PGA Championship

Gallacher used to travel two hours by bus from his Edinburgh home during his school days to take part in junior golf lessons. He set his heart on becoming a professional golfer from an early age and he achieved that goal in 1967. He picked up a mere £953 from his first year as a paid golfer but the following year topped the Order of Merit, thanks to two tournament wins in the British PGA Championship and W.D. & H.O. Wills Open. He also won two events on the Safari Tour.

Ryder Cup debut at 20
Hailed as the new wonder boy of golf at only 20 he was selected for the Ryder Cup team to play the United States at the Royal Birkdale course in Lancashire. The then youngest person ever to play in the series, he displayed tremendous cool in beating no less a mortal than Lee Trevino by 4 & 3 to earn a point in Great Britain's splendid draw.

Bernard played in eight consecutive Ryder Cup matches but was not in the team when Europe won in England in 1985. He did not miss out completely on the triumph because his vast experience was much sought after by captain Tony Jacklin as he became one of the back-room boys.

In 1974 and 1975 Gallacher was the first man to win the coveted Dunlop Masters title in successive years.

For so long the backbone of the Ryder Cup team, Bernard Gallacher was an important member of Tony Jacklin's backroom staff in 1987

Known by his fellow professionals as the Wee Ice Man because of his calm, Bernard has one of the most prestigious club jobs in golf, as the professional at Wentworth, in Surrey. He also diverts a lot of his experience to the PGA of which he is on the Board of Directors of the European Tour. He is also enjoying his time as a course designer and architect, and is involved with the design of a third course at Wentworth.

Bernard may have slipped down the rankings in the last couple of seasons, finishing outside the top 32 in 1986 and 1987, for the first time in his career; but Bernard Gallacher will never be far away from the action because of his sheer love for the game.

'He frightens me with his confidence.'

Peter Alliss about Bernard when he burst on the golfing scene in 1969

LEADING TOURNAMENT WINS

1969
Schweppes PGA Championship
W.D. & H.O. Wills Open

1971
Martini International

1974
Dunlop Masters

1975
Dunlop Masters

1977
Spanish Open

1979
French Open

1982
Martini International
Jersey Open

1984
Jersey Open

DAVID GRAHAM

Born: 23 May 1946, Windsor, New South Wales, Australia

Height: 5 ft 10 in (1.78 m)

Weight: 162 lb (73.5 kg)

Turned professional: 1962

First professional win: 1969 Tasmanian Open

David Graham was the top Australian golfer for many years but now his domination is challenged by Rodger Davis, Peter Senior and Greg Norman

The career of David Graham has certainly been eventful, to say the least. He took up golf at 14 and played left handed. Two years later he became an apprentice professional, and switched to playing with his right hand. He became a full professional at 18 when he took the job at a nine-hole course in Tasmania. Three years later he was declared a bankrupt with debts of more than £3,000. Gradually his golf improved, so did his earning power and he repaid his debts. Since then he has proved himself as a truly international golfer, winning tournaments as far afield as New Zealand, South America, Thailand, South Africa, England, the United States, France and Japan as well as in his home country of Australia.

Family feud

Graham left school much against his father's wishes. He saw no future for his son in golf and his mother had ambitions for David to become a doctor or pilot.

It looked as though his father was going to be proved right, particularly after David's financial problems. David was 24 before it all started to come good. He made the decision to become a regular tournament golfer and played on the Australian, Far East and European circuits. In 1970 he came from obscurity to win the French Open, Thailand Open and then with partner Bruce Devlin to give Australia victory in the World Cup in Argentina. A lot of the credit for David's change in fortunes go to his wife Maureen whom he married in the late 1960s. She calmed David down, as he was often bad tempered and frustrated because he was not making any headway. Maureen's influence also gave David more confidence.

The attack on the States

Those wins, and Maureen's encouragement, inspired him to greater ambitions and in 1971 he set his heart on playing on the US Tour. He came through the qualifying school that year and has been a regular member of the Tour ever since. He has of course made excursions out of the USA which he now regards as home despite retaining his Australian citizenship.

David has won eight times on the US Tour and has been one of the most successful non-Americans on the US circuit. He has certainly been the most successful Australian to play in the USA and in 1983 his career earnings surpassed those of that other great Australian representative on the Tour, Bruce Crampton.

Graham's first Tour win was the 1972 Cleveland Open when he had to beat his close friend and Australian team-mate Bruce Devlin in a play-off. But he had to wait four years before his next win when he took both the Westchester Classic and American Golf Classic to finish eighth on the money-list. That was to herald the start of the best era of his career.

David beat Hale Irwin, going for a hat-trick of wins, at the second extra hole to win the Piccadilly World Match-Play title at Wentworth in Surrey in 1976 and the following year he added the Australian Open and South African PGA titles to his long list of international successes.

It was a relatively barren year in 1978 but a year later he became the first Australian since Peter Thomson to win a major championship when he won the US PGA title at Oakland Hills in Michigan . . . but only just!

At the 72nd hole he needed a four to win the title with a championship record-equalling 63 and beat Ben Crenshaw by two shots. A five would still have given him the title but he took a six and went into 'overtime'. With the odds stacked against him, he kept himself alive at the first two extra holes with successful putts from 18 and 10 feet (5.5 and 3 metres) before winning the title with a birdie two at the third extra hole.

'I'm damned if I know why you haven't won more tournaments.'

Gary Player to David Graham after practising with him before the start of the 1981 US Open

---

A final 18 holes worthy of winning any championship

When he won his second major championship in 1981 he had to come from behind to win and his final 18 holes have been described as the most remarkable in the history of the US Open.

He trailed George Burns by three shots at the start of the last day but then hit every green in regulation for a 67 and one-stroke victory over Burns and Bill Rogers.

In the late 1970s/early 1980s, David Graham became one of the most feared golfers in the world. He has not won on the US Tour since the 1983 Houston Coca-Cola Open and one reason for his demise was his signing of many lucrative endorsements after winning the Open. Consequently his backers needed him for commitments and he spent too much time away from the golf course.

In his younger days in Australia David used to design and build golf clubs in his pro-shop as a means of supplementing his income. He is putting that ex-

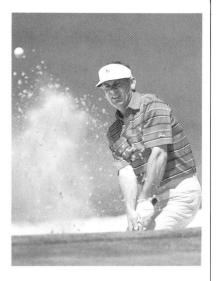

David Graham in action during the 1987 US Masters. He now has his home in the United States

perience to a wider use these days and David Graham-designed clubs are widely used. Even Jack Nicklaus has used his clubs. That is a testament to David's second skill.

LEADING TOURNAMENT WINS

1970
World Cup team (with Bruce Devlin)

1972
Cleveland Open

1976
Westchester Classic
American Golf Classic
World Match-Play
Championship

1979
US PGA Championship

1980
Memorial Tournament

1981
Phoenix Open
US Open

1983
Houston Open

STYLE POINTS

Keeps the ball very low off the tee and with his long irons.

HUBERT GREEN

Born: 28 December 1946, Birmingham, Alabama, USA

Height: 6 ft 1 in (1.85 m)

Weight: 175 lb (79.4 kg)

Turned professional: 1970

First US Tour win: 1971 Houston Open

'I turned pro again' was how Hubert Green summed up his 1985 season. He was making reference to his disastrous two seasons starting in 1982 when his game turned sour on him. In 1983 he slumped to 135th on the rankings. He had, however, been suffering with an injury to his shoulder joints which, at times, meant he was unable to raise his arms above head-height. Nevertheless he carried on playing golf, without complaining. He points out that his game started to deteriorate before the illness and that he was not using the illness as an excuse. He had an operation towards the end of 1983 and in 1984 started modifying his unusual hunched swing. He also changed his grip which improved his short game – a normally outstanding feature, but during his slump it had let him down badly.

Determination pays off

Hard work and the will to win have been a trademark of Hubert Green since his early days as a professional and after the operation, and change of style, he was determined to get back on the winning trail.

He bounced back in 1984 with a leap of 102 places on the ranking list and won the Southern Open, his 18th Tour win, but more significantly, it was his first win for three years.

In 1985 he completed his remarkable comeback by winning his second major championship, the US PGA title at Cherry Hills in Denver, Colorado. He beat off a challenge from Lee Trevino to collect the $125,000 first prize which swelled his season's winnings of more than $230,000 and he was back among the top 20 for the first time since 1979.

A golfing childhood

Green practically grew up on the 12th fairway of the Birmingham Country Club, Alabama. He was the youngest of four children who all played golf and all won local junior tournaments. Hubert

Hubert Green and his wife Karen awaiting the presentation after Green had won the 1985 US PGA Championship at Cherry Hills

'It's been a long dry spell but it's raining up there now.'

After his 1985 US PGA success – referring to the fact that it started pouring down for the presentation ceremony and it was his first win for three years

'I'm not fit to lace up Nicklaus' shoes.'

Often Green's cynical reply to journalists who would mock his unorthodox golf swing

picked up his first golf club when he was five but throughout his school days was a keen all-round sportsman on the insistence of his father who was a strong believer in his children playing as many sports as they could. As years went by Hubert eliminated sports one at a time until he was left with golf.

He went to Florida State University and his game developed strongly during his time there. Although his amateur career was not outstanding, he turned profes-sional in 1970 and got a job as assistant pro at the Merion Golf Club. He qualified for his Tour card in the autumn of that year.

Early professional success

Success came early on in Green's long and illustrious career. He tied the 1971 Houston Open with the experienced Don January, but bir-died the first extra hole to clinch his first title. He finished 29th in the money-list and, not surprisingly, was named Rookie of the Year.

Green had his best ever finish on the money-list in 1974 when he finished third, thanks to victories in the Bob Hope, Greater Jacksonville Open, Philadelphia Open and the Walt Disney World National Team Championship with Mac McLendon. During the mid-70s he became one of the game's most consistent winners and in one amazing three-week spell in 1976 he won three consecutive Tour events, only the tenth man to do so.

Despite his victories and acclaim, he had still not proved himself worthy of being added to the list of all-time greats because he had not won a major tournament. As at the start of the 1977 season, he had won 11 Tour events and nearly $1 million in prize money, but that first big one still eluded him.

Hubert Green in action during the 1985 US PGA. It was only Green's second major in eight years

The elusive major at last

He put the record straight that year by winning the US Open at Southern Hills in Tulsa, Oklahoma. Not only was he under pressure from the world's top golfers on the final day but he had to play after hearing of a death threat. He had the choice to discontinue or complete his round. He decided to play on and at the 18th he had a pressure putt from 3 feet (1-metre) to win the title by one shot from Lou Graham. Normally great with

LEADING TOURNAMENT WINS

1971
Houston Open

1973
Tallahassee Open
BC Open

1974
Bob Hope Classic
Greater Jacksonville Open
Philadelphia Open
Walt Disney World National
Team Championship (with
Mac McLendon)

1975
Southern Open

1976
Doral-Eastern Open
Jacksonville Open
Sea Pines Heritage Classic

1977
US Open

1978
Hawaiian Open
Sea Pines Heritage Classic

1979
Hawaiian Open
New Orleans Open

1981
Sammy Davis Jr–Greater
Hartford Open

1984
Southern Open

1985
US PGA Championship

Hat-trick hero

In 1976 Hubert Green became only the tenth man in US Tour history to win three consecutive events. The following great names achieved the feat before Green: Byron Nelson (twice), Jack Burke, Sam Snead, Ben Hogan, Bobby Locke, Jim Ferrier, Billy Casper, Arnold Palmer and Johnny Miller. This is how Green made up his hat-trick of wins:

1. Doral-Eastern Open
2. Jacksonville Open
3. Sea Pines Heritage Classic

the putter, it did not let him down and the first major trophy was placed on the sideboard at the Green's Florida home.

A month later Green finished third in the British Open at Turnberry in Ayrshire, Scotland, with 279, a score that would have won many a British Open. But he could only sit back and be part of the supporting cast to the two central characters Tom Watson and Jack Nicklaus, who broke Open records galore with their amazing rounds of 268 and 269.

In 1978 Hubert was in line for his second major when, after two middle rounds of 69 and 65 in the US Masters, he led Tom Watson and Rod Funseth by three going into the final round. But Gary Player emerged from the field with a final round 64 to put the pressure on the rest of the leaders. Green led Player by seven at the start of the day and had a 2½-foot (75 cm) putt at the 72nd to force a tie. For once the normally reliable putter let him down. He finished with a 72 and one stroke behind the South African who won his third Masters title.

Green's great friend on and off the Tour is Fuzzy Zoeller. They spend a lot of time together. Zoeller and Green have played together on two Ryder Cup teams, in 1979 and 1985. In the three matches they have played together, they have not won! Green has however, never lost a singles match in his three Ryder Cup appearances (he was also in the 1977 team).

After so many years at the top in the mid-1980s Green began to enjoy family life and spent more time relaxing. Consequently there was a decline in his game in 1986 and 1987, but the previous time he endured a two-year slump he came back by winning his second major and he was not being written off by golf observers.

Green proudly holds the PGA trophy after his two-stroke win over the defending champion Lee Trevino at Cherry Hills Country Club, Denver, Colorado, in 1985 .

HALE IRWIN

Born: 3 June 1945, Joplin, Missouri, USA
Height: 6 ft (1.83 m)
Weight: 175 lb (79.4 kg)
Turned professional: 1968
First US Tour win: 1971 Heritage Classic

Between 1972 and 1985 Hale Irwin won $100,000 in 14 consecutive seasons

Between 1975 and 1978 Irwin won seven Tour events, nearly $1 million and was fourth, third, fourth and seventh on the money-list. That level of consistency made him one of the best golfers of the day.

Talent spotted early
Born in Missouri, Hale still lives in the state, at Frontenac. He went to the University of Colorado where he gained a degree in marketing in 1968. That same year Irwin turned professional and came through the Tour qualifying school in the spring.

His first Tour win came a year later when he won the Heritage Classic. He also broke into the top 20 money-winners and that is where Hale Irwin stayed until 1984, apart from one setback in 1980 when he slipped to 38th place.

Two Opens
The big breakthrough came in 1974 when he won the US Open at Winged Foot, New York, beating the little known Forrest Fezler by two strokes. Three weeks before the Open Irwin dreamt he would win the title. The second great high spot in Irwin's career was five years later when he won his second US Open, this time at Inverness and again by two shots, from Jerry Pate and Gary Player. Irwin's final-round 75 was the highest by an Open champion since 1949.

Popular in Britain, he finished joint second in the 1983 British Open at Royal Birkdale in Merseyside, just one shot behind the winner Tom Watson. During the third round he had a tap-in putt from three inches (seven centimetres). He casually went to knock it in with the back of his putter and missed the ball. It counted one shot and that was the difference between him and Watson at the end of 72 holes.

'Sometimes it stands for Stupid, sometimes for Smart.'

When asked what the 'S' in Hale S. Irwin stood for

Irwin, however, showed great concentration in winning the World Match-Play Championship at Wentworth in Surrey in both 1974 and 1975. He brought an end to the reign of the event's specialist, Gary Player, by beating him 3 & 1 in 1974 and the following year he beat fellow American Al Geiberger 4 & 2. A third successive final appearance followed in 1976 but the hat-trick was thwarted by Australian David Graham who won the final at the 38th hole.

Second only to Nicklaus
Hale's last win on the Tour was the 1985 Memorial Tournament (which he also won in 1983) and it ended a winless 16 months. He had, however, been suffering from a groin strain which occurred on a damp day in the pro-am before the Honda Classic in March 1984. An adjustment to new spectacles in 1985 also slowed down his return to form but once used to them he returned to winning ways. His Memorial triumph was after a great battle with Lanny Wadkins. That was the last season Irwin won over $100,000 but it ended a run of 14 consecutive seasons over $100,000. Only Jack Nicklaus with 16 has enjoyed a longer run of consistency.

Since then Irwin has slipped well down the rankings, largely because outside interests have taken him away from the golf course but in 1986 and 1987 he opened each season with wins, in the Bahamas Classic and Florida Invitational respectively. Both were not official Tour money events but each gave an indication that the fighting spirit of Hale Irwin was still there.

LEADING TOURNAMENT WINS

1974
US Open
World Match-Play Championship

1975
World Match-Play Championship

1979
US Open

TONY JACKLIN

Born: 7 July 1944, Scunthorpe, Lincolnshire, England
Height: 5 ft 9 in (1.75 m)
Weight: 168 lb (76.2 kg)
Turned professional: 1962
First European Tour win: 1967 Pringle Tournament

The playing career highlights of Tony Jacklin are impressive enough, but since he gave up competitive golf he has enjoyed two even greater moments from his long career, in twice leading Europe to victory over the United States in the Ryder Cup.

Jacklin, a stalwart of seven Ryder Cup teams as a player, was honoured with the non-playing captaincy in 1983 when he was given the task of trying to break the US stranglehold, which had last been achieved in 1957. His gallant men came within one point of wresting the trophy at the PGA National, West Palm Beach, Florida. Two years later at the Belfry, Warwickshire, however, he enjoyed one of the greatest moments of his career when he guided the European side to victory and thus ended 28 years of domination by the Americans. Not satisfied with that, however, Jacklin had one other goal – to beat the Americans on their own ground, something that 13 previous British/European teams had failed to do.

On 27 September 1987 at Muirfield Village, Ohio, Tony Jacklin became a national hero once more when he led the European team to a two-point victory over a strong American side.

It was not the first time Jacklin had been hailed as a national golfing hero. Naturally, the same honour was bestowed upon him at the Belfry, Warwickshire, two years earlier; but in 1969 he beat the New Zealander Bob Charles at Lytham, Lancashire, to become the first British winner of the Open since Max Faulkner in 1951.

Riding on the crest of a wave, eleven months later Jacklin added the US Open to become the first Briton since Ted Ray to win the US Open and only the third Briton after Ray and the legendary Harry Vardon to win both titles.

Tony Jacklin was born in Scunthorpe where his father was a locomotive driver at the local steel works and it was in the steel industry that Jacklin started his working life as a poorly paid apprentice. But the lure of golf soon took him away from Scunthorpe to Potters Bar where he became assistant to Bill Shankland. Jacklin was only 17 at the time but he had the opportunity to do what he wanted – play golf.

World-class success

He turned professional at the age of 18 and in 1965 won the Assistant Professionals' title. Two years later he won the Pringle Tournament followed by the pretigious Dunlop Masters to register his first major wins.

Jacklin was convinced he could be a winner in the United States and in 1968 he became the first Briton to win on the US Tour when he won the Jacksonville Open. His British Open success followed a year later and then he won the US Open title. Not only did he beat the best of the Americans at Hazeltine, but he destroyed

them. He led from start to finish and ended up the winner by seven shots from second placed Dave Hill. Tony Jacklin was confirmed as a world class golfer and his rise to the top encouraged youngsters to start playing the game. His appeal was reminiscent of Arnold Palmer's in the United States ten years earlier.

Jacklin won a second Jacksonville Open in 1972 and he kept on winning on the European circuit until 1982 when he won his last title, the Sun Alliance PGA at Hillside. Since then he has become much sought after as a tutor and television commentator, and is one of the most respected men within the sport.

Ryder Cup delights

Having won the British and US Open titles Jacklin could never have believed he would top those two great moments for sheer excitement but winning the Ryder Cup at the Belfry and then beating the Americans on home soil surpassed his own individual triumphs. When he won at Lytham and Hazeltine, while he had the whole nation behind him, he was winning the titles for himself. In the two Ryder Cup victories he had the nation behind him once more, but this time he was winning *for* them. When he was speechless after winning the Cup in 1987 his genuine emotions brought a lump to many a throat around Britain and Europe.

Tony Jacklin has done more for British golf since the mid-1960s than any other man. He has not only been the inspiration behind the success of many of today's leading players, but his successes in the early 1970s were instrumental in many of them taking the

sport up in the first place. Jacklin's contribution to golf has not gone unrewarded and he received the OBE for his services to golf and the PGA have made him an honorary member.

When he is not winning Ryder Cups Tony Jacklin spends his time at the Las Aves Club in Sotogrande, Spain.

'I never thought I would live to see golf played the way it was today.'

After the 1987 Ryder Cup win

'This could change the course of world golf.'

Again after the 1987 Ryder Cup win

Opposite page: Tony Jacklin enjoying the first 'greatest moment' of his career after winning the 1969 British Open.
Left: Jacklin relishing another, after leading the European team to win the Ryder Cup on American soil in 1987

LEADING TOURNAMENT WINS

1967
Dunlop Masters

1968
Jacksonville Open

1969
British Open

1970
US Open
Lancôme Trophy

1972
Jacksonville Open
PGA Championship

1973
Dunlop Masters

1982
PGA Championship

BETSY KING

Born: 13 August 1955, Reading, Pennsylvania, USA

Height: 5 ft 6 in (1.68 m)

Weight: 124 lb (56.3 kg)

Turned professional: 1977

First US LPGA Tour win: 1984 Women's Kemper Open

After seven years on the US LPGA Tour without a win Betsy King eventually broke her duck in March 1984 when she won the Kemper Open at Kaanapalli, Hawaii.

Since then she has been one of the biggest money-winners on the US Ladies' Tour and has not stopped adding to her list of victories. She has been a winner every year since 1984 and at the end of 1987 had totalled 11 Tour wins. In those four years she had won over $1 million and twice been the top money-winner.

Promising amateur

She reached the semi-final of the US Junior Championships at the age of 17 and in 1976 was a National Collegiate Champion with the Furman University team. She was also the best placed amateur, in eighth place, in that year's US Ladies' Open. Betsy turned professional in 1977.

Before her first Tour win in 1984 King had come close several times to picking up the winner's cheque, and particularly in the 1979 Wheeling Classic when she was beaten in a play-off by Debbie Massey. But it all came right for Betsy in 1984.

She came to Britain for the Ladies' Open in 1985 and carried off the first prize at Moor Park in Hertfordshire with a brilliant four iron to within 5 feet (1.5 metres) of the pin at the 72nd to give her a hat-trick of birdies in the last three holes to clinch victory by two strokes from Spain's Marta Figueras-Dotti. The following year Betsy had her best ever chance of winning the US crown until a double bogey six at Dayton's 14th on the final round lost her the lead she looked like holding on to. A final-round 75 lost her the title by one stroke, with Jane Geddes winning after a play-off with Sally Little.

That disappointment was forgotten in 1987 as she won three Tour events, including her first major, the Nabisco Dinah Shore.

A professional since 1977 and one of women golf's biggest money-winners Betsy King did not win her first major until 1987 when she won the Nabisco Dinah Shore

LEADING TOURNAMENT WINS

1985
British Ladies' Open

1987
Nabisco Dinah Shore

TOM KITE

Born: 9 December 1949, McKinney, Texas, USA
Height: 5 ft 8 in (1.73 m)
Weight: 154 lb (69.9 kg)
Turned professional: 1972
First US Tour win: 1976 IVB-Bicentennial Golf Classic

Tom Kite may not have won any of golf's four major titles but he is the third biggest money winner of all time and since joining the US Tour in 1972 has won more than $3 million. That highlights the level of consistency of this great player.

One of the best players not to have won a major

If any man deserves a major tournament win it is Kite. He finished second, along with three other men, behind Jack Nicklaus in the 1978 British Open at St Andrews. It was also Nicklaus who destroyed Kite's chances in the 1986 US Masters just when it looked as if that elusive major was coming his way. However, Nicklaus stormed through with a 65 to win by one shot. Kite and/or Greg Norman looked likely winners on the final day until the Nicklaus storm. Tom still had a chance to level on the 18th but missed an 11-foot (3.4-metre) putt.

It was the second time Kite had finished runner-up in the US Masters, the other occasion being in 1983 when Spaniard Seve Ballesteros won by four shots from Kite and Ben Crenshaw.

Top money-winner

Disregard the winning of a major championship as the measure of success and Tom Kite has been one of the most successful US players since the late 1970s. He has won over $100,000 in 12 consecutive seasons and has not finished outside the top 25 money-winners since 1974, when he was 26th. He has won ten Tour events since opening his account in the IVB-Bicentennial Classic in 1976 and in

1981 he reached the summit of his career by topping the money-list, ending Tom Watson's four-year reign at the top, and was named the US PGA's Player of the Year. In 26 starts that year Tom had an outstanding 21 top-ten finishes. He was also the Vardon Trophy winner with a stroke average of 69.80 – the fifth best of all time.

He retained the Vardon Trophy the following year with a stroke average of 70.21 and missed the cut only once in 25 starts. When he did miss it, in the Canadian Open, it ended a sequence of 53 tournaments without missing the 36-hole cut.

Success at an early age

The success bespectacled Kite has enjoyed was anticipated. He started playing golf at the age of six when his father put a club in his hand and insisted he had a swing with it. Five years later he won his first golf tournament and when he was 14 he started taking the game seriously. In 1970 he was beaten into second place in the US Amateur Championship, one stroke behind Lanny Wadkins, and the following year went on to represent his country in the Walker Cup. He was a member of the victorious US Team in the Eisenhower Trophy in Madrid that year and in 1972 shared the NCAA title with Ben Crenshaw while at the University of Texas.

He turned professional in 1972 and was the US PGA's Rookie of the Year for 1973 when he missed only three cuts all season. Although he had to wait until 1976 for his first win, he was already

Just love the hat . . . Tom Kite in action during the 1987 US PGA Championship at the PGA National

LEADING TOURNAMENT WINS

1976
IVB-Bicentennial Golf Classic

1978
BC Open

1981
Inverrary Classic

1982
Bay Hill Classic

1983
Bing Crosby National Pro-Am

1984
Doral-Eastern Open
Georgia Pacific Atlanta Classic

1985
Tournament of Champions

1986
Western Open

1987
Kemper Open

'Golf is not like tennis, or basketball, or football where you can control your opponent. With golf you cannot control your opponent. If Jack misses a couple of putts I win the tournament. But he didn't, did he? We did!'

Referring to Jack Nicklaus's 'stealing' the 1986 US Masters when both Kite and Greg Norman could have, or should have, won the title

Never a 'major' but runner-up three times		
1978	*British Open*	
281	Jack Nicklaus	
283	Ben Crenshaw	
,,	Ray Floyd	
,,	Tom Kite	
,,	Simon Owen	
1983	*US Masters*	
280	Severiano Ballesteros	
284	Tom Kite	
,,	Ben Crenshaw	
1986	*US Masters*	
279	Jack Nicklaus	
280	Tom Kite	
,,	Greg Norman	

showing a high level of consistency and in his third full year had pulled himself to 18th on the money-list, yet he was still waiting for a win.

Since winning however, he has become one of the most feared men on the US circuit and since 1979 has been a regular member of the Ryder Cup team. His level of consistency in that competition

Above: Tom Kite in action during the 1986 US Masters
Below: Kite putting in the final round. He finished tied second, and is still without a major

matches his all-round play.

As Kite started the 1988 season he was the only player on the US Tour to have recorded a win every season since 1981.

BERNHARD LANGER

Born: 27 August 1957, Anhausen, West Germany

Height: 5 ft 9 in (1.75 m)

Weight: 156 lb (70.8 kg)

Turned professional: 1972

First European Tour win: 1980 Dunlop Masters

Bernhard Langer is undoubtedly the best player ever to have come out of Germany and in recent years has been one of the best to have come from Europe. With Spaniard Severiano Ballesteros he has been vying for the title of Europe's top golfer since 1980.

The pendulum has slightly swung towards the Spaniard but on his day Langer is the better player, not only in Europe but also on the United States circuit where he has shown his true worth by winning twice on the US Tour, including the Masters.

Langer switches his season between the two circuits and is a successful money winner on both.

Child caddie to adult pro

Langer's first involvement with golf was as a nine-year-old caddie when he used to walk five miles (eight kilometres) to the Augsburg Club near his home town of Anhausen. Within a couple of weeks he decided he wanted to play and announced that he was going to

Above: Bernhard Langer in the 1987 Ryder Cup
Below: Langer at the 1986 British Open

International winner

A truly international golfer, Bernhard Langer has won major tournaments in

Australia	Ireland	Scotland
Colombia	Italy	South Africa
England	Japan	Spain
France	Netherlands	USA
		West Germany

Langer being fitted with the Masters' green jacket in 1985

play the game for a living one day. Golf was not a popular sport in Germany and he was laughed at. Between then, and when he left school at 15, he would play, practice and caddie whenever he could. He then turned professional (in 1972) and became the assistant to Heinz Fehring at the Munich Golf and Country Club. Fehring was Langer's first coach.

Unsure at first whether he wanted to be a teacher or tournament player, he eventually set out for the European Tour when he had completed his apprenticeship at 18. In 1976 he contracted the dreaded 'yips', the curse of all players. Happily they eventually went.

He won the 1979 World Under-25 Championship by a massive 17 strokes after rounds of 73 and three 67s, and followed that with his first Tour win a year later when he captured the Dunlop Masters, the first German to win a major professional tournament. In 1981 he won the Bob Hope British Classic and then became the first German

winner of the German Open, a proud moment for Bernhard. He was second to Bill Rogers in the 1981 British Open at Sandwich, Kent. He ended the season as the top money-winner in Europe. Ryder Cup selection followed and he has been a member of the European side ever since.

Langer's putting problems reappeared in 1982. The problem was cured again and he finished second in another British Open when his rival Ballesteros beat him at St Andrew's in 1984. He was top money-winner for a second time in 1984 and also played on the US Tour. He won $82,000 and did enough to secure his Tour card.

LEADING TOURNAMENT WINS

1980
Dunlop Masters

1985
US Masters
Sea Pines Heritage Classic
Australian Masters
European Open

1986
Lancôme Trophy

1987
Irish Open
White & Mackay

Making it on the US Tour

Although he was receiving rave notices in Europe, Langer still knew that he could not be regarded as a truly great player until he proved himself on the US Tour. He did just that in 1985 when he won the US Masters after coming from being six behind the leaders at the half-way stage to shoot two brilliant 68s, including four birdies in the final seven holes, to win by two from Curtis Strange, Ray Floyd and Seve Ballesteros. That win at Augusta in Georgia was followed a week later with victory in the Sea Pines Heritage Classic when he beat Bobby Wadkins at the first extra hole in the play-off at Harbour Town, South Carolina.

Ballesteros–Langer rivalry

The rivalry between Langer and Ballesteros has been intense over the years and never more so than in the Suntory World Match-Play championship at Wentworth. They have met in the final twice, and both times victory has gone to the Spaniard, first in 1984 by 2 & 1 and a year later by 6 & 5.

Langer has, however, had his moments of glory, particularly at Augusta in 1985 when the title of Best European Golfer swung from Spain to West Germany. The two players were victorious team-mates in the 1985 and 1987 Ryder Cups.

Although Bernhard's putting has been his 'worst enemy' at times, when it is working he is one of the best players in the world and so difficult to beat.

STYLE POINTS

Pulls the club through the ball with his strong left-hand grip. Not text-book, but effective.

NANCY LOPEZ

Born: 6 January 1957, Torrance, California, USA	
Height: 5 ft 5 in (1.65 m)	
Weight: 125 lb (56.7 kg)	
Turned professional: 1977	
First US LPGA Tour win: 1978 Bent Tree Ladies' Classic	

With over $2 million in winnings Nancy Lopez is one of the top women golfers in the United States

Nancy Lopez has been one of the top names in women's golf since turning professional in 1977 when she finished second in the US Open, her first professional event. She has won over $2 million from golf.

A very promising amateur

Nancy started playing golf at the age of eight under the guidance of her father Domingo. As an amateur her record was outstanding: she was the New Mexico Amateur champion at 12, US Junior Girls' champion twice, Western Junior champion three times and was the Mexican Amateur champion in 1975, when she also tied for second place in the

US Open. Nancy gained representative honours with the US Curtis Cup team and played in the World Amateur Team Championship. Her transition to the professional game was half-way through the 1977 season but her exploits in finishing second in the Open and European Open at Sunningdale in

Berkshire gave a pointer as to what the world of women's golf could look forward to.

The promise fulfilled

In her Rookie season, 1978, she won nine Tour events including an astonishing five in succession. She won the US LPGA title by six strokes and pocketed a record $189,000, a figure no player had ever reached in a Rookie season at the time. She won both the Player and Rookie of the Year awards. She was top money-winner again in 1979 and was the first woman to win over $200,000 in a season.

Problems with her game started in 1980, a hook appeared in her drive and the previously devastating putting skill deserted her. She had married sports commentator Tim Melton in 1979 but the marriage eventually broke up and Nancy married Ray Knight, who played for the New York Mets baseball team when they won the 1986 World Series, and more recently of the Baltimore Orioles, in October 1982. Nancy missed part of the 1984 season to give birth to

their first child, Ashley Marie, and part of 1986 for an encore – she gave birth to their second child Erinn Shea. In between, she managed to win the US LPGA title for a second time and top the money-list for the third time with a record (by more than $100,000) $416,472. She also shot a US LPGA record four-round total 268 in winning the Henredon Classic.

She was inducted into the Hall of Fame in 1987 after winning her 35th Tour event, the Sarasota Classic, Florida, and over 500 people saluted her at the induction ceremony at Tiffany's, New York, including President Reagan.

LEADING TOURNAMENT WINS

1978
US LPGA Championship

1985
US LPGA Championship

'When do you want me to start, and where do you want me to be?'

Caddie Dee Darden after being invited to caddy for Nancy in the 1987 Open nearly two years after they went their separate ways. Darden caddied for Nancy during her successful 1985 season

---

STYLE POINTS

A long driver and a bold putter, she attacks the hole with each putt.

DAVIS LOVE III

Born: 13 April 1964, Charlotte, North Carolina, USA	
Height: 6 ft 3 in (1.91 m)	
Weight: 175 lb (79.4 kg)	
Turned professional: 1985	
First US Tour win: 1987 Heritage Classic	

LEADING TOURNAMENT WINS

1985
Walker Cup

1987
Heritage Classic

'I started playing golf as soon as I could walk', says Davis Love III, and for somebody playing that long, together with an expert tutor like his father, it was an even-money bet he would make the grade as a professional.

> **'That day, something told me I belonged.'**
>
> *Referring to his playing alongside Ben Crenshaw in the 1986 Tournament Players' Championship*

Early ambitions
Since he was nine years old all he has wanted to do is play golf. Davis was brought up in a golfing environment; his father, Davis Love junior, was a tournament professional and the mark III version used to travel to tournaments with him. He met great players and from an early age felt he wanted to do nothing with his life but play golf.

His father, for many years regarded as one of the game's leading coaches and technicians, built a swing for his son at an early age. The swing has remained unaltered and it has enabled him to get distance as well as accuracy. He was the leader on the 1986 Tour driving statistics with an average of 285.7 yards.

Educated at the University of North Carolina, he was three times

Davis Love III won his first event on the US Tour in 1987 when he took the Heritage Classic

the All-American champion and the 1984 American College Champion. He was honoured with selection for the US Walker Cup team in 1985 and shortly afterwards turned professional and immediately had no problem coming through the US Tour qualifying school. The decision to turn professional was certainly the right one because a new star was unearthed. His first season on the US Tour saw him in with a chance in the Canadian Open and Buick Open but he let it slip at the last minute.

A little help from a friend
Davis gives a lot of credit for his first year success to Ben Crenshaw, his playing partner in the 1986 Tournament Players' Championship at Sawgrass in Florida.

He won his first Tour event in 1987 when he took the Heritage Classic after Steve Jones dropped two shots on the last hole to hand victory to Love. Second-year earnings were in the region of $300,000 as he finished in the top 30.

STYLE POINTS

Generates a lot of clubhead speed as a result of a very high arc through taking the clubhead well above his head.

SANDY LYLE

Born: 9 February 1958, Shrewsbury, Shropshire, England	
Height: 6 ft 1 in (1.85 m)	
Weight: 187 lb (84.8 kg)	
Turned professional: 1977	
First European Tour win: 1979 Jersey Open	

When Sandy Lyle won the $180,000 first prize in the richest ever US Tournament Players' Championship at Sawgrass, Florida in 1987, Ken Schofield, the executive director of the European PGA described it as the greatest moment for British golf on the US Tour since Tony Jacklin's 1970 US Open win.

Lyle had already won on the US Tour, when he took the Greater Greensboro Open the previous year, but he proved his ability to live with the best of the American players at Sawgrass by beating Jeff Sluman at the third extra hole in a play-off. Lyle proved to the US fans that he was a worthy member of the US Tour which he had been playing since 1984.

Dad's influence
The credit for Sandy Lyle's success story belongs to his father Alex, the professional at Hawkstone Park in Chepstow, on the Wales–England border, since 1955. It was under his guidance and inspiration that Sandy developed into the fine golfer he is today. Golf had been in the family even before Alex because Sandy's grandfather built the Clober course at Milngavie on the outskirts of Glasgow, even though he wasn't a player himself.

When he was ten Sandy broke 80 for the first time and, despite his love of soccer at the time, told his father he wanted to be a professional golfer. Alex did nothing but encourage his son. They struck a deal; Alex said that if he was a scratch golfer by the time he was 15 he would help him. Sandy made it, and with a few years to spare! He would be seen on the golf course before going to school. As a youngster he developed a flat round swing which, if you look closely, you can still see signs of.

Top junior
Sandy was picked for the English Boys' team when he was 14 and at 17 he won the English Amateur Stroke-Play championship. He gained the title in 1977 and won the British Youths' Championship the same year. He culminated his last year as an amateur by representing Great Britain in the Walker Cup against the United States. He turned professional later in 1977 and the following year had his first win as a professional when he won the Nigerian Open, posting a round of 61 along the way. Perhaps inevitably, he was the Rookie of the Year for 1978.

The following season Sandy topped the European money-list after wins in the Jersey Open, Scandinavian Enterprise Open and the European Open. He was top money-winner again in 1980 and between 1979 and 1985 never finished lower than fifth on the Order of Merit; he was the top money-winner for the third time in 1985. He slipped down the list in 1986 and 1987 because he concentrated on the US Tour, where he more than compensated for his lack of European earnings.

Britain's first Open winner since Tony Jacklin in 1969, Sandy Lyle after winning in 1985 at Royal St Georges

A great British triumph

Sandy Lyle has enjoyed many great moments from golf but his greatest day was in 1985 at Royal St Georges in Kent when he became the first Briton since 1969 and only the third since 1951 to win the British Open.

He was three shots off the lead after three rounds. His swing wasn't quite right and his putts weren't dropping but then suddenly, it all came together in the final round and birdies at the 14th and 15th set up a one-stroke win over American Payne Stewart.

'It relieved me of one of my mental problems.'

After winning the Greater Greensboro Open in 1986 (he had won on most golf circuits but felt he had to win in the United States)

'I thought motorbikes were dangerous, but that really scared me.'

Winning the White Horse Golfer of the Year title in 1982 meant that Sandy had to ride a white horse through London's Piccadilly when he collected his prize!

'I am surprised it has taken him so long to win it.'

His father on Sandy's eventual triumph in the British Open

STYLE POINTS

One of the game's longest hitters, particularly with his long irons. Perfect takeaway.

Lyle's victory in the Open was a hard act to follow but a couple of months later he was a member of the European Ryder Cup team that defeated a US team for the first time since 1957. Since then, however, apart from his two wins on the US Tour, little seemed to be right for Sandy, and his personal problems did not help matters. The Open win took a lot out of him, mentally and physically.

Towards the end of 1987 things started looking up for Sandy. Firstly he was a member of the victorious Ryder Cup team then, a couple of weeks' later, he beat the local hero Bernhard Langer to win the German Masters at Stüttgart.

Sandy has been a member of every Ryder Cup team since 1979 and in 1980 he won the individual title at the World Cup when he helped Scotland to second place.

For his achievements and services to golf Sandy was awarded the MBE in 1987.

A very thoughtful Sandy Lyle during the 1987 US Open

MARK McCORMACK

Born: 1931, USA

Mark McCormack warrants inclusion for his contribution to the sport not as a great player but as the proprietor of the biggest sports management agency in the business.

McCormack's International Management Group now also markets tennis players, skiers, racing drivers, but his association with sport started with golf and with one golfer in particular: Arnold Palmer.

The early McCormack-Palmer connection

McMormack graduated from Princeton in 1954 with a degree in law. He was a keen and useful golfer at the time and played in the British and US Amateur Championships and once in The US Open.

Palmer and McCormack were team-mates on the Wake Forest University golf team and both went on to become legends. When Palmer started setting the golf world alight in the late 1950s and early 1960s with play never seen before, his old school pal McCormack saw a marketable commodity. People were expressing a great interest in golf, and in particular that interest came from the average man in the street. McCormack set the marketing wheels in motion and so was born a great partnership. The rest of the Mark McCormack story is legend, as he sought and got control over the world's top sportsmen and women and marketed them as superstars.

In the 1960s McCormack had control over Palmer, Nicklaus and Player. They became known as the Big Three and McCormack played a big part in securing lucrative endorsements and contracts for them. The television exposure he arranged for them helped to popularize golf on both sides of the Atlantic.

Described as the 'most powerful man in professional sport', his International Marketing Group was the forerunner of the many sports agencies that have sprung up in recent years. It still remains the most powerful.

An outstanding businessman, his book *What They Don't Teach You at Harvard Business School* was a best-seller, as is his annual *World of Professional Golf* which is a requisite of any golf statistician's library.

Mark is not only one of the top marketing man, but also, has picked up valuable golfing experience over the years and his knowledge of the game is put to use behind the microphone where he is one of the summarizers for BBC Television.

Leading agent Mark McCormack . . . obviously he's got a deal in mind involving the Eiffel Tower!

MARK McNULTY

Born: 25 October 1953, Bindura, Rhodesia (now Zimbabwe)
Height: 5 ft 10 in (1.78 m)
Weight: 158 lb (71.7 kg)
Turned professional: 1977
First European Tour win: 1979 Greater Manchester Open

Mark McNulty has certainly earned himself a reputation as the play-off specialist. When he beat Scotland's Sam Torrance with a 40-foot (12-metre) putt at the second extra hole to win the 1987 *London Standard* Four Stars event at Moor Park in Hertfordshire it was the 13th play-off of his professional career, and was his 13th win.

He came through the same Salisbury (now Harare) golfing school as current professionals Denis Watson and Nick Price.

Disasters

McNulty has been plagued by injuries and disaster since he turned professional in 1977. In 1980 he survived a car accident when his car hit a bus near his parent's farm in Zimbabwe. A couple of weeks earlier a close friend, the leading South African golf writer Adrian Frederick, suffered severe brain damage in a car accident.

Despite his setbacks, Mark McNulty, famous for his splendid collection of white caps reminiscent of that other great South African Bobby Locke, has developed since the mid-1980s into one of the most consistent golfers on the European and South African circuits. In 1987 he went through one spell of winning 11 tournaments from 18 starts.

American failure, European success

Like his two fellow countrymen Mark spent time on the US Tour but in 1985 he left and returned to Europe. Because of a back injury he did not play enough US tournaments and lost his Tour card. (It was later discovered that his long-standing back trouble stemmed from his right leg being almost ½ inch [11-mm] shorter than his left.

During his first full season back on the European Tour he finished a personal best sixth on the money-list and took his European earnings past the £100,000 mark. He also won the Portuguese Open, his first European win for six years, and he gave his prize money to Adrian Frederick.

In 1987 McNulty won successive tournaments, the *London Standard* and then the £33,000 prestigious Dunhill British Masters after surviving a fighting charge from Ian Woosnam. He completed a hat-trick of wins by winning the German Open with a score of 259, clipping one shot off Kel Nagle's 26-year-old European Tour record.

Zimbabwe's Mark McNulty shakes hands with Ian Woosnam after McNulty's one-stroke win over the Welshman in the 1987 Dunhill British Masters

LEADING TOURNAMENT WINS

1980
German Open

1986
Portuguese Open

1987
Dunhill British Masters
German Open

JOHN MAHAFFEY

Born: 9 May 1948, Kerrville, Texas, USA	
Height: 5 ft 9 in (1.75 m)	
Weight: 160 lb (72.6 kg)	
Turned professional: 1971	
First US Tour win: 1973 Sahara Invitational	

American John Mahaffey has been a professional since 1971. He won the US PGA title in 1978 when he beat Tom Watson and Jerry Pate after a three-way tie. Since then he has not won a major but in 1986 he won the prestigious Tournament Players' Championship

John Mahaffey cured a problem in 1986, and as a result he won the Tournament Players' Championship at Sawgrass in Florida. Well, he didn't strictly win it, rather Larry Mize gave it to him.

Mize, known for his self-destruction, was three shots up with four holes to play. Somehow he lost the championship and the $162,000 first prize to Mahaffey after missing a 3-foot (1-metre) putt on the 18th green to force a play-off. Mahaffey won by one and it was a testament to him that he should play a consistent final round and snatch the title because his putting had been impeccable.

Mahaffey concentrated on taking his game more seriously. It paid dividends and he finished the season with personal best winnings of $378,172, and took his career earnings past $2 million.

John Mahaffey had left the amateur game with a fine record behind him. He was the 1970 NCAA Champion for the University of Houston. He turned professional in 1971 and joined the Tour that same year. Unlike many youngsters who joined the Tour, Mahaffey did not have a powerful drive. He was, however, a good striker of the ball and very accurate. He has since altered his swing to give him that extra length but without losing the accuracy.

Since 1972 he has been consistently among the top 50 money-winners except in 1977 when he slumped to 150th as a result of damaged tendons in his left elbow which started to give him trouble during the 1976 US PGA Championship at the Congressional course in Maryland. The year before Mahaffey had served notice of his ability when he tied with Lou Graham in the US Open at Medinah, Illinois, although it was Graham who won the play-off by two strokes over 18 holes.

From seven behind to win the PGA title

Once the elbow was better, Mahaffey was back among the money-winners in 1978 and he won his first major by coming from seven behind Tom Watson in the final round to win the US PGA title at Oakmont in Pennsylvania after beating Watson and Jerry Pate in a play-off. He concluded the year with his third win on the Tour by taking the American Optical Classic, and by helping the United States to win the World Cup (with Andy North) as well as winning the individual title. Mahaffey finished 12th on the money list with a then personal best $153,520 . . . $144,600 more than he won in 1977.

Since then John has won the World Cup team title a second time (with Hale Irwin), the Bob Hope twice, the Kemper Open, Anheuser–Busch Classic, the Texas Open and, of course, the Tournament of Champions. He also serves the US PGA Tour on the Tournament Policy Board of Directors.

When John Mahaffey's game is right there are few golfers who can strike the ball with the same authority. That insurance he took out when he changed his swing to get more distance out of his drive is paying dividends and he looks like being a regular money-winner on the Tour for several years to come.

LEADING TOURNAMENT WINS

1978
US PGA Championship

1985
Texas Open

1986
Tournament Players Championship

STYLE POINTS

Consistently drives straight down the middle of the fairway.

JOHNNY MILLER

Born:	29 April 1947, San Francisco, California, USA
Height:	6 ft 2 in (1.88 m)
Weight:	182 (82.6 kg)
Turned professional:	1969
First US Tour win:	1971 Southern Open

Johnny Miller, the winner of the 1976 British Open at Birkdale

Nineteen-year-old Johnny Miller signed up to caddie when the 1966 US Open came to his home course, the San Francisco Olympic Club in California. He decided he might as well have a try at qualifying. Remarkably he did so, finished all four rounds in the tournament proper and was the best placed amateur in eighth place.

The new golden boy arrives
That success story was the start of the great career of golf's golden boy of the 1970s.

Miller started playing golf at the age of five and was the US Junior Champion in 1964. He graduated from Brigham Young University in 1969 with a degree in physical education. A protege of fellow Mormon Billy Casper, he qualified for the US Tour that spring and within two years had won his first event, the Southern Open, by beating the current Tour commissioner, Deane Beman, into second place.

Johnny Miller really arrived when he shot a final-round championship record 63 to win the 1973 US Open at Oakmont in Pennsylvania to take the title by one stroke from John Schlee. That heralded the start of three glorious and successful seasons for the new glamour boy of US golf.

A successor to Nicklaus?
Naturally, he was hailed as the next Jack Nicklaus and his domination of the sport in 1974 had very few doubting such a claim. Standing over 6 foot (1.8 metres), he had a very upright swing and could hit the ball long and straight, both off the tee and with irons.

He started the year in a blaze of glory winning the Phoenix Open with a score 24-under par. The following week he completed one of the most remarkable feats of consecutive scoring on the US Tour when he won the Tucson Open with a score of 25-under par. In each tournament he recorded a round of 61.

Eight tournament wins that year placed him at the top of the money-list with a record $353,021. Nicklaus regained the position in 1975 but Miller still won four Tour events and was second in the money-list.

Although 1976 saw him drop to 14th on the US Tour Johnny made a big impression in England by winning the Open at the Royal Birkdale course in Merseyside after a great battle with the then unknown Seve Ballesteros. Miller won in the end by six strokes from the Spaniard and Jack Nicklaus who shared second place.

Ballesteros' collapse in the final round was reminiscent of Miller's demise in the 1971 US Masters when he led by two with four to play before losing to Charles Coody, who played the last four holes in two-under par to win the tournament from Miller and Nicklaus.

Down, but not out
After his successful years Miller rested on his laurels, having obtained the financial security he had sought, and between 1977 and 1979 was without a win. His complacency, together with his desire to spend more time with wife Linda and their six children were the main factors in his decline. However, a revival followed in 1981 when he won the Tucson and

LEADING TOURNAMENT WINS

1973
US Open
World Cup (team and individual)

1974
Tournament of Champions
World Open

1975
World Cup (team and individual)

1976
British Open

1979
Lancôme Trophy

1981
Sun City Challenge

STYLE POINTS

One of the many upright swingers. Note how upright he is after the follow-through.

'It's one thing to beat the young guys, but when you beat Jack, and on national television, it's real sweet.'

After beating Nicklaus to win the 1983 Honda Inverrary Classic

Los Angeles Opens. He was twelfth on the money-list and in South Africa he landed golf's first $500,000 cheque when he won the Sun City Challenge. The revival continued in 1982 and 1983 but the curtailment of tournaments after that saw him slump to 118th in 1986.

However, the one-time golden boy of world golf returned in 1987 to win the AT&T National Pro Am at Pebble Beach in California with some of the more recent big names of golf, Payne Stewart, Lanny Wadkins and Bernard Langer in close pursuit. The first prize of $60,000 helped to swell the already fat Johnny Miller bank balance.

His career earnings from more than 25 tournament wins worldwide are over $3 million and in the United States he is one of the top 20 money-winners of all time.

Miller is a great believer in the family and devotes a lot of time to his own and to his religion. He values his family, religion and golf as the three most important things in his life. If one had to go he says, unhesitatingly, it would be golf.

'The best thing that ever happened to me was coming second in the 1971 Masters. I couldn't have coped if I'd won.'

Commiserating comments to Severiano Ballesteros after the Spaniard had thrown away his chance of winning the 1976 British Open at Birkdale. Miller suffered a similar disappointment in the 1971 US Masters, but appreciated it did him no harm. The same can now be said of Seve.

Johnny Miller, 1986 style. In the mid-1970s he was seen as the man to topple Nicklaus but, after two years at the top, he slipped away

LARRY MIZE

Born: 23 September 1958, Augusta, Georgia, USA

Height: 6 ft (1.83 m)

Weight: 160 lb (72.6 kg)

Turned professional: 1980

First US Tour win: 1983 Danny Thomas–Memphis Classic

As spectators looked up towards the top of the leader board during the 1987 US Masters you could hear them saying 'Larry who?' as they saw the name of Larry Mize. At the end of 72 holes and two extra play-off holes, the golfing world knew only too well who Larry Mize was.

'Nobody wanted to win the US Masters – Mize did.'

An eminent golfing critic after the 1987 US Masters

A dream fulfilled

He was the man born a 'nine-iron shot' from the famous Augusta National course in Georgia, the permanent home of the US Masters championship. As a youngster he used to dream of sinking the winning putt to take the Masters. He was the one who used to write to the management committee asking for a job at the Masters each year and who eventually got one, tending to the leader board. Little did he really think his name would be at the top of it one day, but it certainly was and there was nobody more surprised than Larry himself. It was so unexpected, he didn't have a shirt and tie to wear for the presentation dinner in the evening and PGA officials had to go out and buy him one. Larry's wife Bonnie had to go home to change into an evening dress!

Local hero Larry Mize (right) after receiving the Masters' green jacket in 1987 from the defending champion Jack Nicklaus

Larry Hogan (a family name) Mize started playing golf at the age of nine under the guidance of his father, a marketing manager with a telephone company and a scratch golfer himself. Larry had few lessons in his early years, and is virtually self-taught, but has a classic swing. After an undistinguished amateur career he joined the US Tour in 1982 and reminded spectators of the young Tom Watson. He won his first tournament, the Danny Thomas, in dramatic style, by holing a 25-foot (7.5-metre) putt on the last green to take the title.

When he won the Masters four years later, it was also in dramatic fashion. At the second extra hole of the play-off with Greg Norman (Seve Ballesteros was also in the play-off, but was eliminated at the first extra hole) he played a dream of a chip from 140 feet (43 metres) to clinch victory.

Winning the Masters did not affect his game as sometimes happens but, in contrast, gave him more confidence. And he ended the season as a member of the US Ryder Cup team. No longer do golf fans have to ask 'Larry who?' when they see his name shoot towards the top of the leader board.

LEADING TOURNAMENT WINS

1983
Danny Thomas–Memphis Classic

1987
US Masters

STYLE POINTS

Not one of the biggest hitters but an accurate driver.

TSUNEYUKI 'TOMMY' NAKAJIMA

Born: 24 October 1954, Gumma, Japan	
Height: 5 ft 11 in (1.8 m)	
Weight: 175 lb (79.4 kg)	
Turned professional: 1975	
First major professional win: 1977 Japanese PGA title	

When Tommy Nakajima was in with a chance of winning the 1986 British Open, and becoming the first Japanese golfer to win one of the world's four major tournaments, millions of people in Japan sat up until the early hours of the morning watching their hero in action on television.

For three rounds he pushed Greg Norman before handing victory to the Australian. Nakajima started the final round one shot behind tournament leader Norman but three-putted from 6 feet (1.8 metres) at the first hole of the final round. He never recovered from that disaster and finished down the field in eighth place after a 77.

'I'm, now a very good friend of sand.'

Tommy's comments during the 1986 British Open when he was reminded of his exploits at the 1978 US Masters and British Open

---

Disasters . . . nothing new to Tommy

Disaster has followed Tommy in the majors throughout his career, and few people need reminding what a dreadful three months he had in 1978. First, in the US Masters at Augusta in Georgia he found sand at the 13th and took 13 shots to complete the hole. Three months later at St Andrews he found sand at the infamous Road Hole when he was among the leaders in the Open. He took four to get out of the bunker and completed the hole in nine shots, by which time he had slid well down the leader board.

Tommy took a while to recover from those disasters. He had always been a strong driver but

In 1986 Tommy Nakajima became the first player to win 100 million yen

seemed to be packing even more power into his drives as if he was anxious to get birdies out of every hole. It didn't work. He lost his accuracy and his game fell apart.

His new wife Ritzuko, older, and perhaps wiser than Tommy, became his calming influence. She talked him out of his bad spell and he got his game back together again and has since emerged as the top Japanese golfer in succession to Isao Aoki.

Bespectacled Tommy started playing golf at the age of nine and his only teacher in those early days was his father. He became the youngest ever winner of the Japanese Amateur title at 18. He still

regards that as the greatest accomplishment of his golfing career. He turned professional two years later, in 1975, and has since won more than 30 professional events on the Japanese circuit.

Tommy, real name Tsuneyuki, but often known as 'Sands of . . .' because of his surname, had his heart set on playing in the United States since his early days as a professional, and in 1983 he joined the US Tour. He never finished higher than 77th on the money-list but he values highly the experience he picked up. He made a lot of friends there, and improved the best features of his game, his driving and long-iron play.

He did not retain his US Tour status in 1986 because he failed to fulfil tournament requirements. He returned to the Japanese circuit and won the money title for the third time in four years and became the first to win over 100 million yen in one season, despite making occasional excursions to play in Britain. He is remembered for his epic battle with Sandy Lyle in the Suntory World Match-Play Championship at Wentworth in Surrey which Lyle won in overtime, by snatching victory at the second extra hole after both had shot great rounds of 65 and 64.

LEADING TOURNAMENT WINS

1973
Japanese Amateur Championship

1977
Japanese PGA Championship

1983
Japanese PGA Championship

1984
Japanese PGA Championship

1985
Japanese Open

1986
Japanese Open

LARRY NELSON

Born: 10 September 1947, Fort Payne, Alabama, USA
Height: 5 ft 9 in (1.75 m)
Weight: 154 lb (69.9 kg)
Turned professional: 1971
First US Tour win: 1979 Jackie Gleason–Inverrary Classic

Larry Nelson with the US PGA Championship Trophy in 1987. He won the same title six years earlier

Larry Nelson had ambitions of being a baseball or basketball star as a youngster. He attended the Southern Tech for a year before being called up. After his military service, he returned to further education for a while and got a job as an illustrator.

A late starter

He first hit a golf ball in 1969 at the age of 22, at a local golf range. He enjoyed it so much he got himself a job in Bert Seagreaves' pro shop at the Pine Tree Club, Georgia. He turned professional shortly afterwards, in 1971, but had to play the mini-tours before getting his Tour card in 1973.

'Just to let the other one know it can be replaced.'

When asked why he carried two putters in his bag

A great competitor with a fluent swing, Nelson had to wait six years for his first victory but he immediately followed with a second win and suddenly he was one of the hottest properties in golf. He finished the 1979 season runner-up in the money-list with $281,022, second only to Tom Watson. He was chosen for the US Ryder Cup team in 1979 and won all five matches he played. He played four matches in the 1981 Ryder Cup and won them all.

He won the first of his three major tournaments in 1981 when he won the US PGA Championship by four strokes from Fuzzy Zoeller in front of thousands of his home fans at the Atlanta Athletic Club in Georgia.

Return from the wilderness . . . part 1

In 1983, when it seemed a decline in his game had set in, he came from nowhere to win the US Open at Oakmont, near Pittsburgh in Pennsylvania. Even after two rounds he was seven off the lead but he then had a 65 and virtually won the tournament with a 62-foot (19-metre) putt for a birdie at the 70th hole, to set up a one-stroke victory over Tom Watson.

A born-again Christian, Larry is the Minister of the US Tour's Bible Study group. One of his travelling companions for the 1983 British Open at Birkdale was fellow religious devotee Rollen Stewart. Seen by millions of television fans during the four days coverage, Stewart was easily identifiable as the man with the purple, blue, yellow and red wig. Sadly there was no divine intervention because Larry finished joint 53rd, 13 shots off the winner.

Return from the wilderness . . . part 2

After winning the Walt Disney World Golf Class in 1984 Larry Nelson did not win anything until the 1987 US PGA Championship at Palm Beach Gardens in Florida. Then he came from the wilderness once more to beat Lanny Wadkins at the first sudden-death hole. Poor putting had been the reason for his three-year slump but everything slotted into place at Palm Beach Gardens and this victory ensured Larry a third Ryder Cup selection. Larry's win in the PGA ended a series of 18 majors in which no player had won more than once. That run started when Larry won the Open in 1983.

LEADING TOURNAMENT WINS

1981
US PGA Championship

1983
US Open

1987
US PGA Championship

STYLE POINTS

A stylist with a slow deliberate takeaway and backswing, and beautiful rhythm. When putting forms a perfect V stemming from his hands opening out at his shoulders, and with his elbows tucked into his body.

JACK NICKLAUS

Born: 21 January 1940, Columbus, Ohio, USA	
Height: 5 ft 11 in (1.8 m)	
Weight: 182 lb (82.6 kg)	
Turned professional: 1961	
First US Tour win: 1962 US Open	

Who is the greatest-ever golfer? Was it Braid, Taylor or Vardon? What about Hagen and Bobby Jones? Then there was Sam Snead and Ben Hogan, followed by Arnold Palmer. And of course, there is Jack Nicklaus.

Comparisons from different eras are impossible, and unfair. Each of those was a giant in his own right.

At the top for 25 years

Nicklaus, nicknamed the Golden Bear, is the biggest money-winner the sport has seen with total earnings of more than $5 million, and his 71 US Tour wins is second only to Sam Snead's 84. Furthermore his 18 professional major tournament wins is seven more than the next best man, Walter Hagen. Add two US Amateur titles to that list and there is some justification for the claim that Nicklaus is the greatest golfer of all time.

He has been at the top for 25 years and between his first year as a professional, 1962, and 1978 his lowest position on the US money-list was fourth! He was the top winner eight times and in the 16 consecutive seasons 1963-78 he topped $100,000 a season. There was a slight decline in the mid-1980s when he cut back on his Tour schedule, but in 1986, at the age of 46, he showed the band of up-and-coming youngsters that there was still a lot of golf left in the 'old-timer' as he won the US Masters for a record sixth time.

A lucky break

The son of a pharmacist, Jack stumbled across golf by accident and so did his father Charles. His father injured an ankle playing basketball when Jack was ten. The ankle was put in plaster and he was told to walk between two and three miles a day as physiotherapy. Nothing was said about not playing golf so he took the sport up and Jack used to accompany him as his caddie. Jack fell in love with the game straight away and it was not long before he became Jack Grout's star pupil at the Scioto Country Club in Columbus, Ohio.

The USA's top amateur . . .

At 15 Nicklaus appeared in his first US Amateur championship but lost in the first round to Bob Gardner. At 16 he won the Ohio Junior Championship and the Ohio State Open with a four-round total 282. In 1959 he won

Jack Nicklaus (right) and Tom Watson at the end of one of the best-ever British Opens, at Turnberry in 1977. Watson won by one stroke.

the US Amateur at Broadmoor, in the foothills of the Rockies. He holed an 8-foot (2.4-metre putt for a birdie three at the last hole to dethrone Charlie Coe. Nicklaus became the second youngest winner and later in the year he gained Walker Cup honours.

Jack won the NCAA Championship and his second US Amateur title in 1961, and gained a second Walker Cup selection. In between his two amateur titles he played on the winning US Eisenhower Trophy winning team, and was also the winner of the individual title.

He was still an amateur when he finished second to Arnold Palmer in the 1960 US Open at Cherry Hills and was still undecided whether to turn professional. He married in July 1960 and had set his heart on becoming a pharmacist like his father. He held an apprentice pharmacist's licence for a while, but the lure of golf was too great and he turned professional in 1961.

'Can you get him to stop talking, we've a plane to catch.'

Wife Barbara's pleas to newsmen when Jack just wouldn't stop talking after winning the 1978 Open at St Andrews

'I kept hearing people talk about "the kid" and "the veteran". This is the first time I was ever classed a veteran and I still can't get used to it.'

On being called a veteran at 26 when he was playing with 19-year-old Johnny Miller during the 1966 US Open

'OK! where do you want me to start, 1959?'

As he walked into the press tent after winning the 1986 US Masters

'I used to use three a round but since I bought the company I only use one.'

Referring to his gloves, and subsequent acquisition of the Macgregor company

. . . *becomes a top professional*

Within a year he had turned the tables on Palmer by beating him in a play-off to win the US Open at Oakmont, near Pittsburgh in Pennsylvania. In 90 holes of golf Nicklaus three-putted only one green. That was Nicklaus's first Tour win and he went on to win on the Tour every year until 1979.

Master of the Masters

Nicklaus has loved the big occasions and he is never more at home than at the National course at Augusta, Georgia, the home of the US Masters Tournament. Even today, he still starts the event as one of the favourites.

He has made the US Masters *his* event, and has won the title six times. His first success was in 1963 when he beat Tony Lema by one

Nicklaus in action at his favourite course, Augusta, in the 1985 US Masters. The following year he won the title for a record sixth time

shot but when he won in 1965 he beat his two great rivals and contemporaries, Arnold Palmer and Gary Player, by an astounding nine strokes. He needed a play-off against Gay Brewer and Tommy Jacobs to retain the title a year later but when he won for the fourth time in 1972 he had a three-shot lead over Tom Weiskopf, Bobby Mitchell and Bruce Crampton.

Nicklaus won a record fifth Masters in 1975 in what has often been described as the best Masters

of all when he won by one from Tom Weiskopf and Johnny Miller. His most pleasing win, however, was in 1986 when he beat a strong international field including great winners like Spaniard Seve Ballesteros and Australian Greg Norman to snatch a one-stroke victory.

International success

Apart from wooing fans in the United States Nicklaus has found friends in golfing countries all over the world, particularly in Australia and Britain.

He has won the Australian Open six times but another reason why he likes Australia is because he can partake in his favourite pastime – fishing – there. Shortly before winning the 1978 Australian Open he caught a monster 600-pound

Two of golf's all-time greats, Jack Nicklaus and Arnie Palmer, paired during the 1987 US Masters at Augusta

(275-kg) black marlin off Cairns, Queensland.

British fans first had a glimpse of the youngster's rare talent when he played at Hillside, Southport in 1962. Since then he has been a popular visitor to British shores. What is more, he has been a regular winner, having won the Open three times. One Open he will be particularly remembered for was at Turnberry in Scotland in 1977 when he and Tom Watson broke British Open records galore as they matched each other hole-for-hole over four days. Watson eventually won by one shot.

LEADING TOURNAMENT WINS

1962
US Open

1963
US Masters
US PGA Championship

1965
US Masters

1966
US Masters
British Open

1967
US Open

1970
British Open

1971
US PGA Championship

1972
US Masters
US Open

1973
US PGA Championship

1975
US Masters
US PGA Championship

1978
British Open

1980
US Open
US PGA Championship

1986
US Masters

STYLE POINTS

An upright golfer who stands behind the ball and lines up his target before addressing the ball. But the most important point to watch in Jack is his temperament – he never seems to lose his cool!

Jack's first British Open success was at Muirfield in Scotland in 1966. He regarded the course as one of the fairest in championship golf and when he built his own course at Columbus, Ohio, he called it Muirfield Village. The course was used for the 1987 Ryder Cup when Jack was the non-playing captain of the US team for the second time.

Nicklaus was seen as the man to win back the cup for the Americans. Pride had been dented at the Belfry two years' earlier under Lee Trevino's leadership. Now, over Jack's own course, he had the difficult job.

However, Tony Jacklin's team proved too much for Jack's and the United States lost on home soil for the first time. Jack, generous in defeat as ever, was the first to congratulate Jacklin and admit the better team won.

The businessman

When he is not playing golf Jack runs his business empire, Golden Bear Inc.

Over the years he has been involved in many successful ventures, but two disastrous property deals have cost him dearly.

Now , most of his time is spent designing golf courses for which he charges $1 million per course!

One of the biggest kicks Jack has had in recent years has been in watching his two sons, Jack and Gary, establish themselves as fine golfers. Jackie in particular has taken great strides and is showing potential consistent with the Nicklaus name.

Such is the appeal of Nicklaus that when he won the 1986 US Masters with the Macgregor ZT big-headed putter, sales of the putter grossed $11 million in a year. If people copy Jack Nicklaus in other ways, apart from his golfing style, then they will not go too far wrong. He epitomises all that is good in sport and whoever it was that once said: 'Jack Nicklaus is a good winner, but a superb loser' just about summed up the great man.

All-time US career money winners (as at end of the 1987 season)		
Jack Nicklaus	$4,976,981	1962-87
Tom Watson	$4,701,630	1971-87
Tom Kite	$3,445,007	1972-87
Ray Floyd	$3,372,340	1963-87
Lee Trevino	$3,315,503	1966-87

In she goes . . . Nicklaus holes a vital putt at the 17th on his way to winning his record sixth Masters title in 1986

GREG NORMAN

Born: 10 February 1955, Mount Isa, Queensland, Australia

Height: 6 ft 1 in (1.85 m)

Weight: 182 lb (82.6 kg)

Turned professional: 1976

First professional win: 1976 West Lakes Classic (Australia)

If you look at Greg Norman's winnings from the US Tour in 1987 you would say he had a good year. Although he did not add to his total of four Tour wins he still won over $500,000 and was among the top 10 money-winners. But that was failure compared with a remarkable 1986 season.

Top man in the States, nearly top in Europe

Norman has always set himself high standards but even he was astounded at his level of success in 1986. He was the top money-winner in the United States with $653,296 and the second highest money-winner in Europe, behind Ballesteros, with £224,373.

He won the Las Vegas Invitational and Kemper Open (for a second time) on the US Tour and won the British Open, European Open and Suntory World Match-Play title (for a third time) on the European circuit. Additionally, on returning to his native Australia he won three tournaments in a row, to end a remarkable season. That impressive list of successes could have been even greater if he had not 'thrown away' three majors.

So nearly four majors

No-one has ever won all four major championships in one year. Ben Hogan won three in 1953, but in 1986 Norman came the closest any man has to winning all the titles, when he led the four championships going into the final round, only to see victory disappear in three of them.

Jack Nicklaus deprived him of the US Masters with a majestic final-round 65 and in the US Open at Shinnecock Hills on Long Island Ray Floyd took the title from Norman after the Australian shot a final-round 75. Victory eventually came for Greg in the Open at Turnberry in Scotland when he won by five shots from Britain's Gordon J. Brand after a blistering second-round 63. Yet another near miss came in the US PGA championship at Inverness in Ohio when victory looked certain. This time he lost by two strokes to Bob Tway.

Norman has had a reputation over the years for not being able to clinch victories. That was never more evident than in his performances in the three American major tournaments in 1986.

A late starter

Norman did not take up golf until he was 16. At school he had played Rugby League and Australian Rules Football. He came across golf only by chance when he caddied for his mother Toni, a 3-handicap player, at the Virginia Golf Club in Brisbane. When she completed her round he borrowed

'I've got a major at last' . . . Greg Norman after winning the Open Championship in 1986

her clubs and hit a few balls. Within two years he was a scratch golfer.

Although he did not try to copy Jack Nicklaus, a lot of his early instruction came from reading two books written by the great man. He learnt from an early age the need to hit the ball long from the tee and he was advised by his first coach, Charlie Earp, to forget accuracy, which would follow in time. That was sound advice as Norman became one of the biggest hitters in

STYLE POINTS

Powerful from the tee, because at impact his weight is on his left leg and his head is still behind the ball.

golf.

He turned professional in 1976 and when he won his first tournament, the West Lakes Classic in Adelaide, a lot of people took notice because the field contained such notable Australians as Graham Marsh, Bruce Devlin,

Bruce Crampton and David Graham.

He joined the European Tour the following year and finished 20th on the order of merit thanks to winning the Martini International. The signs of Norman's true quality were beginning to show in 1980

when he won the French and Scandinavian Opens before taking the World Match-Play title at Wentworth by beating Sandy Lyle by one hole. He won the Martini International for a third time in 1981 and also the prestigious Dunlop Masters. By now he was establishing himself as a truly international golfer, having finished fourth in the US Masters at Augusta in Georgia. There was another important event in the life of Greg Norman in 1981, he married wife Laura, a former American Airlines flight attendant.

Wins in the Dunlop Masters, State Express Classic and Benson & Hedges International put Greg top of the 1982 European Order of Merit. However, there was one event Grey will wish to forget from 1982. In defence of his Martini International title at Lindrick in Yorkshire he took a 14 at the par-four 17th! In 1983 he shared his tournament play between Europe and the United States and ended

Left: Greg Norman lining up a putt at a windy St Andrews during the 1986 Dunhill Cup. Representing Australia, Norman, along with David Graham and Rodger Davis, won the title by beating Japan in the final

Below: Greg Norman beat Sandy Lyle to win the 1986 Suntory World Match-Play Championship at Wentworth. It was Greg's third win in the event and Sandy's third defeat. Greg is seen with his two children Morgan-Leigh, and Greg Jnr – in the trophy!

LEADING TOURNAMENT WINS

1980
French Open
Australian Open
Scandinavian Open
World Match-Play Championship

1981
Dunlop Masters

1982
Dunlop Masters

1983
World Match-Play Championship

1984
Canadian Open

1986
British Open
World Match-Play Championship

the season with a second World Match-Play title, beating Nick Faldo 3 & 2 in the final.

'I shot a few when I became irritated because they were eating my fish.'

Norman clarifying the stories that abounded about him shooting sharks in his younger days

'It was a wonderful feeling walking up the 18th. I couldn't see anything but the backs of people's heads.'

Norman ruefully describing his 'victory' walk up the 18th fairway on his way to winning the 1986 British Open

---

The American challenge

Greg became a regular US Tour member in 1984. He had first played in the USA in 1977 when he competed in the Memorial Tournament and in 1981 he attracted a lot of attention in the US Masters, not only for his golf, but also for his stories about shark-hunting. It was after that he was given the nickname the great white shark because of his stories and blond hair.

By 1984 he was ready to attack the US golf circuit seriously. In his first full season on the Tour he won the Kemper and Canadian Opens to reach ninth on the money-list. He nearly won the US Open at Winged Foot, near New York, when he came from behind and holed a 40-footer (12 metres) on the 72nd to force a play-off with

Fuzzy Zoeller but he was drained for the next day's 18-hole play-off and lost by eight shots.

That near-miss was more than compensated for when he won the British Open two years later when, apart from receiving the congratulations of thousands of fans, he was congratulated by many of his fellow professionals who thought the win was deserved and long overdue. Among them was Jack Nicklaus, the man he has been likened to so many times.

Australian Greg Norman in action during the 1987 US PGA Championship at the PGA National. In 1986 Greg was in contention for all four majors going into the final round

CHRISTY O'CONNOR, JNR

Born: 19 August 1948, Galway, Republic of Ireland	
Height: 5 ft 11 in (1.8 m)	
Weight: 170 lb (77.1 kg)	
Turned professional: 1967	
First European Tour win: 1975 Carrolls Irish Open	

Christy O'Connor Jnr

It cannot have been easy for O'Connor to follow in the footsteps of his famous uncle and namesake but he has been a consistent campaigner in Europe for nearly 20 years. He also proudly carried the name of Christy O'Connor to the top of the leader board in the 1985 British Open.

Christy O'Connor junior had been playing on the European Tour for 15 years before he became a so-called overnight success. Although a steady player and consistent money-winner he had never finished higher than seventh on the Order of Merit, which he achieved thanks to two wins in 1975, but in 1985 he won £68,693, beating his previous seasonal best by more than £44,000.

LEADING TOURNAMENT WINS

1974
Zambian Open

1975
Carrolls Irish Open
Martini International

1976
Sumrie Better-Ball (with Eamonn Darcy)

1978
Sumrie Better-Ball (with Eamonn Darcy)

1984
Zambian Open

'It was a great apprenticeship. He is the biggest single influence in my golfing life. I will be forever in his debt. He taught me everything.'

On his famous uncle whom he joined as assistant at Royal Dublin in 1967

'He'll have heard about it right enough – but it's just rather nice to be doing some more justice to his name, isn't it?'

After his record 64 in the 1985 Open . . . referring to his uncle, of course

A 64 at St Georges but no championship

Although he didn't register a win in his record season he finished third in the Dutch and Sanyo Opens and in the British Open at Royal St George's at Sandwich in Kent. Then it looked after the first round as if he was going to do something his famous uncle, Christy senior, never did in his long career, and win the coveted title.

O'Connor opened the 114th Open with a course record 64, shattering Henry Cotton's 51-year-old record, but a second round 76 was to be his downfall.

Despite two closing rounds each of 72 he was two shots behind the winner Sandy Lyle and finished joint third, collecting £23,600 in the process. Christy's 64 was, however, the lowest score by a British Isles competitor in British Open history. It won him the Tooting Bec Cup, a trophy his famous uncle had won in 1961, 1963 and 1969.

Christy had a great spell in mid-season and was fully expected to make the 1985 Ryder Cup team, ten years after his first and only appearance, but he fell away badly towards the end of the season. The season ended on a note of personal tragedy for Christy because his father (Christy senior's brother) died. He was about to pull out of the Irish World Cup team after the tragedy but his uncle made him play for his father's sake.

One of the biggest thrills in Christy's career was winning the 1975 Carrolls Irish Open at Woodbrook, revived after 22 years, when he won with a four-round total of 275, which stood as a new record for the event until bettered by Seve Ballesteros at Royal Dublin in 1983. Surprisingly Christy senior never won the Irish title.

STYLE POINTS

A very straight driver but his best 'style' point is his famous white cap!

MAC O'GRADY

Born: 26 April 1951, Minneapolis, Minnesota, USA

Height: 6 ft (1.83 m)

Weight: 165 lb (74.8 kg)

Turned professional: 1972

First US Tour win: 1986 Greater Hartford Open

One of the most colourful characters on the US Tour, Mac O'Grady turned professional in 1972 but he did not come through the qualifying Tour school until ten years and 17 attempts later!

Born Phil McGleno, he changed his name to Phillip McClelland O'Grady in 1978. The McClelland was after Bob McClelland, a man who had been like a father to him for years, and O'Grady was his mother's maiden name. The family moved to Los Angeles when he was nine, and when he was 12 he started caddying. Some of the businessmen he used to caddie for eventually became his sponsors as he sought to get on the professional Tour.

sophical remarks often difficult to comprehend, about the game of golf and life in general.

Mac's wife Fumiko is Japanese, and they both practise yoga. But what about his golf . . .

He never broke into the top 100 during his first two years on Tour, 1983 and 1984, but the next year he

came close to victory in the Las Vegas Invitational, Buick Open and Byron Nelson Classic but still collected $223,000 and climbed to 20th place in the rankings. He won $33,000 more the following season, and enjoyed his first Tour win, but slipped to 26th.

The first win was in dramatic style. He shot a final-round 62 to force a play-off with Roger Maltbie in the Greater Hartford Open and then won with a birdie at the first extra hole.

> **'I've played so many places round the world during the last 10 years or so, being on the Tour is like celebrating Christmas every day.'**
>
> *On eventually coming through the Tour school*

> **'One minute the sword is making you king, the next it is lacerating you.'**
>
> *O'Grady's homespun wisdom, referring to the putter*

> **'If you can bring the ship home with cargo and crew intact through the hurricane of the last day, that's an achievement. Right?'**
>
> *In answer to 'How did that 65 compare with your 62 in the Greater Hartford Open?' Ask O'Grady the time and he will tell you how the watch works*

The best win of his career was in the second event of the 1987 Tour, the Tournament of Champions at La Costa, San Diego. He opened with a 65 and held on with some nervy putting for a final-round 71 and a one-shot win over Rick Fehr.

A non-conformist, O'Grady was suspended by the US PGA because of 'conduct unbecoming a golf player'. He responded in 1987 by issuing a writ for $12 million damages against Tour commissioners Deane Berman and the US PGA.

For relaxation Mac enjoys his time marathon running and used to spend a lot of his time running up and down Malibu beach.

LEADING TOURNAMENT WINS

1986
Greater Hartford Open

1987
Tournament of Champions

The most unconventional Mac O'Grady . . . both on and off the golf course. On it, he plays right-handed but putts left-handed. Off the course he has had a few skirmishes with the golfing authorities

Extrovert

He is certainly the extrovert of the Tour. Ambidextrous, he plays right-handed to the green and then putts left-handed. He is constantly coming out with zany philo-

——— STYLE POINTS ———

Unorthodox, but achieves great distance with his drives.

JOSE-MARIA OLAZABAL

Born: 5 February 1966, San Sebastian, Spain
Height: 5 ft 10 in (1.78 m)
Weight: 154 lb (69.9 kg)
Turned professional: 1985
First European Tour win: 1986 Ebel European Masters–Swiss Open

LEADING TOURNAMENT WINS

1986
Ebel European Masters–Swiss Open
Sanyo Open

Between 1983 and 1985 Spain's Jose-Maria Olazabal proved himself the leading amateur golfer in Europe. When he topped the European PGA qualifying school at La Manga in December 1985 the new professional was already receiving rave notices. But even the fondest of admirers couldn't have imagined that he would have opened his Rookie season with two Tour wins and finish second on the Order of Merit behind countryman Severiano Ballesteros with £155,000 – three times more than any other Rookie had won.

One of the heroes of the 1987 Ryder Cup, Jose-Maria Olazabal (right) taking advice from mentor Seve Ballesteros.

> **'I have studied Olazabal in action and he has impressed me as a young man whose outstanding talent promises a great future.'**
>
> *Triple British Open champion Henry Cotton*

The hottest property in Europe

Olazabal, whose father and grandfather were both greenkeepers, started playing golf at the age of four with a cut down club. By the time he was 15 he was playing off scratch and at 17 he was the Italian and Spanish amateur champion, as well as the British Boys' champion. He followed that with wins in the British Amateur championship in 1984 and the British Youths' Amateur championship the following year; the first time anybody had won all three British titles.

Then came the Tour school at La Manga when he led from start to finish to win by two shots and get himself on the 1986 Tour. A lot of credit for Jose-Maria's great amateur career goes to tutor John Jacobs who helped him change and perfect his swing in 1983.

Even Ballesteros, who hails from just along the northern Spanish coast from Olazabal's San Sebastian home, could not boast such a great start to his professional career. Olazabal tied second place with Ronan Raffety, behind another Spaniard, Antonio Garrido, in the 1986 *London Standard* tournament at Moor Park in Hertfordshire but three months later he won his first title when he captured the Ebel European Masters–Swiss Open with a 26-under par total of 262 thanks to rounds of 64-66-66-66. A month later he beat Howard Clark by three shots to win the Sanyo Open

at El Prat in Barcelona to register his second win, and become the first Rookie since Gordon Brand Jr in 1982 to win two major titles.

When he first joined the professional ranks he was hailed as the second Seve but he refutes such a claim, acknowledging Ballesteros as a genius who cannot be copied. Olazabal regards himself as a steady player who can be as good as Seve one day. He maintains his inspiration did not come from Ballesteros because he had wanted to become a professional golfer long before Seve's rise to stardom.

Despite failing to get on the list of winners in 1987 he still managed to maintain his level of consistency which is remarkable for somebody so young and he was one of Tony Jacklin's three preferences for a Ryder Cup place. He did not disappoint and, with Ballesteros, won three of his four doubles.

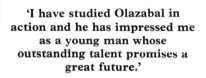

STYLE POINTS

Exemplary with the wedge and on the putting surface.

MARK O'MEARA

Born: 13 January 1957, Golsboro, North Carolina, USA
Height: 6 ft (1.83 m)
Weight: 182 lb (82.6 kg)
Turned professional: 1980
First US Tour win: 1984 Greater Milwaukee Open

A tremendously naturally gifted golfer, Mark O'Meara rose dramatically to the top in 1984 as a result of meeting teaching professional Hank Haney two years earlier. Houston-based Haney added that little bit of refinement to his game.

LEADING TOURNAMENT WINS

1984
Greater Milwaukee Open

1985
Bing Crosby Pro-Am
Hawaiian Open

1986
Australian Masters

1987
Lawrence Batley International

Second only to Watson
O'Meara tended to have an upright swing but Haney taught him to understand the mechanics of the golf swing and a few minor adjustments turned O'Meara into a more consistent golfer. The hours of hard work spent with Haney paid off when O'Meara finished just $10,000 behind Tom Watson at the head of the US money-list in 1984. Although he won only one tournament, the Greater Milwaukee Open, he was second five times, third three times and

American Mark O'Meara has shown he can win on the European Tour as well as the US circuit

finished in the top ten on 15 occasions.

Despite following that great season with two more Tour wins he never quite maintained that same level of consistency but was still tenth on the 1985 money-list. He achieved his one Ryder Cup selection the same season.

Mark started playing golf when he was 13. The family moved from North Carolina to Mission Viejo, California. Their house was next to a golf course and as Mark didn't know any kids in the area he used to spend his time on golf.

Golf scholar
He earned a golf scholarship and went to Long Beach State University. He climaxed a great amateur career by winning the Mexican, California State, and US amateur titles. He beat John Cook 8 & 7 in the final of the Amateur Championships.

From 1980 to 1987 O'Meara won approaching $1½ million on the US Tour, and added to these earnings by winning tournaments in Japan and Australia. He won the Lawrence Batley International at Royal Birkdale in 1987 with a course record 271, four better than Tom Watson's winning score in the 1983 Open over the same course. Just as he did when he won the Australian Masters, O'Meara had two eagles in the final round but this time they were eagle twos, and both with seven irons. What is more, he was trying out a brand new set of clubs! The man acting as caddie for him that day, was Hank Haney.

STYLE POINTS

Has a fluent and precise swing. More often than not will draw off the tee but fade with his irons.

ARNOLD PALMER

Born: 10 September 1929, Latrobe, Pennsylvania, USA

Height: 5 ft 10 in (1.78 m)

Weight: 180 lb (81.7 kg)

Turned professional: 1954

First US Tour win: 1955 Canadian Open

On 10 September 1979 the peace and solitude of the US Seniors Tour was shattered by the arrival of Arnold Palmer. The man who had been the scourge of professional golfers during the 1960s was back to torment his former rivals once more. Having reached the age of 50 he was not just going to let the closing days of his golfing career gently pass him by, but wanted to be a winner again. In the eight years since he joined the Tour he has done just that, and at the age of 58 is a much feared golfer once more.

Palmer the player

The son of a former professional, Palmer first picked up a golf club when he was three years old. When he was 17 he won the Western Pennsylvania Amateur, his first golfing title. After three years serving in the US Coastguards and winning a scholarship from Wake Forest University the Arnold Palmer success story started when he won the 1954 US Amateur title after beating Robert Sweeney by one hole in the final.

Palmer turned professional the following year and earned the first of his $2 million-plus career earnings when he collected $145 for finishing 25th in the Fort Wayme Open. Palmer was on his way and it was not long before the first of his 61 US Tour wins arrived on a sweltering day at Toronto when he won the Canadian Open.

Little did the ten thousand golf fans realize that day that they were witnessing the coming of golf's next 'Messiah' – Arnold Palmer. Basking in 100°F (38°C) sunshine, Palmer shot a final-round 70 for a four-round total of 265, 23-under par, to beat Jack Burke by four shots and collect the winner's cheque of $15,000.

That was to herald the start of a great career that is measured not only in tournament successes but by the contribution made to the game as a whole by Palmer.

Between 1957 and 1971 Palmer never finished out of the top 10 money-winners in the United States and was the top winner on four occasions. In honour of his achievements the leading money-winner on the US Tour since 1981 has been presented with the Arnold Palmer Award.

Palmer was at the peak of his career in the 1960s and was the most exciting player in the world to watch. Although his swing was unorthodox he was a great putter.

Arnie Palmer with his wife after winning his first Open Championship at Birkdale in 1961

He may be a bit older and wiser, but the love of the game has never waned for Arnold Palmer

He was not a stylish putter, but was so confident on the putting surface that he totally dominated the ball.

If there is one tournament Palmer has a special affection for it is the US Masters always played at the Augusta National course in Georgia. He has won the title four times and the famous 'Arnie's Charge' was never more evident than when he last won the title in 1964. Rounds of 69, 68, 69 and 70 gave him victory by six strokes from his great rival Jack Nicklaus.

That was Palmer's last major but in 1966 he had the chance of winning his second US Open when, with nine holes to play, he led Billy Casper by seven shots. He bogeyed the 10th with a five, and at the 16th his tee shot hit a tree. He took two to get out of the rough, his fourth went into the bunker, he was on the green in five and down for a bogey six. He bogeyed the next and, as Casper had been picking up birdies along the way, the two men were all square. They each made par-fours at the 18th but in the play-off the next day it was Casper's confidence that was sky-high and he ended up the winner by four shots.

This was a reverse of what happened when Palmer won the US Open at Cherry Hills in Denver, Colorado, six years earlier, coming from being seven behind to win the title. On that occasion the unfortunate golfer was Mike Souchak, who started the final round on 208. Palmer was well down the field on 215 but he opened with four consecutive birdies as he blitzed his way to an outward 30. Three more birdies on the back nine saw him win by two shots from the young amateur Jack Nicklaus.

Of the four majors, Palmer has never won the US PGA title; the closest he came was in 1968 when he finished one stroke behind the 48-year-old winner Julius Boros.

Since joining the US Seniors Tour his famous band of loyal supporters, 'Arnie's Army', have continued to follow him, and they have witnessed him win most of the major honours available in the seniors' game.

'It was pretty damned similar . . . I lost all three!'

When asked how his play-off defeat in the 1966 US Open compared with his play-off defeats in 1962 and 1963

'Being paired with Palmer is like a two-shot penalty.'

John Schlee during the 1973 US Open

'I ever I had an 8-foot [2.4-metre] putt and everything I owned depended upon it, I'd want Arnold Palmer to take it for me.'

One of golf's greats, Bobby Jones, himself an admirer of Arnold Palmer

Palmer as golf's popularizer

Palmer did not have a classic swing, and at times looked awkward, but he was still successful. Suddenly, the average club golfer was identifying himself with this new phenomenon. Ever increasing numbers of people started playing

LEADING TOURNAMENT WINS

1955
Canadian Open

1958
US Masters

1960
US Masters
US Open

1961
British Open

1962
US Masters
British Open

1963
World Cup (team)

1964
US Masters
World Match-Play
Championship

1966
Australian Open

1967
World Match-Play
Championship

1975
British PGA Championship

1980
US PGA Seniors
Championship

1981
US Senior Open

1984
US PGA Seniors Tournament
Senior Tournament Players'
Championship

1985
Senior Tournament Players'
Championship

golf and the sport grew in popularity as a participant and spectator sport.

Along with Mark McCormack, Palmer was responsible for promoting the sport by taking it to the masses, both live and via television. In turn it attracted spon-

sors, which in turn brought vast sums of money into golf which are now commonplace.

Apart from playing on them, Arnie designs golf courses: the Bay Hill course at Orlando, Florida, is one of his works. The Hertz Bay Hill Classic is played over the course and is known as Arnie's Tournament. Palmer won the tournament once, in 1971, when he shot a championship record 270.

The man who has been the inspiration to thousands of golfers, Arnold Daniel Palmer

Palmer as promoter of the Open
Palmer also played a large part in reviving American interest in the British Open Championship. Undoubtedly the most famous golfing tournament in the world, it lost its international appeal in the mid-

---

STYLE POINTS

Pulls the clubhead through the ball when driving. Very strong hands.

Fifteen years running as a top ten money-winner

Between 1957 and 1971 Palmer was never lower than tenth on the money-list in the United States. This is how he fared season-by-season:

1957	5th	$28,803	1962	1st	$81,448	1967	2nd	$184,065
1958	1st	$42,608	1963	1st	$128,230	1968	7th	$114,602
1959	5th	$52,462	1964	2nd	$113,203	1969	9th	$105,128
1960	1st	$75,263	1965	10th	$57,770	1970	5th	$128,853
1961	2nd	$61,091	1966	3rd	$110,467	1971	3rd	$209,603

1950s but with Palmer's arrival on the golf scene he was determined to restore it to its rightful place in the golfing world. In 1960 he led the US invasion that has not since waned, and the record of American players in the championship has been second to none since then.

Palmer finished second to Kel Nagle on his Open debut, but in 1961 he won the first of two consecutive titles when he beat Britain's Dai Rees by one shot at the Royal Birkdale course in Lancashire. The following year he destroyed the field at Troon in Scotland and won by six strokes.

A legend in his lifetime

Arnold Palmer is still one of the game's most charismatic players. He has been idolized on golf courses the world over: at one stage at the peak of his career he was reckoned to be the most identifiable man on earth! There is even an Arnold Palmer Tea Shop in Japan.

Golf fans who have seen him play must always be grateful for that opportunity and golf professionals must always remember that they owe Arnold Palmer an enormous debt.

Arnold Palmer getting ready for action in the 1984 US Masters at Augusta. He didn't win the title but his presence attracted just as much interest as the day he first played in the tournament in 1958

JERRY PATE

Born: 16 September 1953, Macon, Georgia, USA

Height: 6 ft (1.83 m)

Weight: 175 lb (79.4 kg)

Turned professional: 1975

First US Tour win: 1976 US Open

What's this, Jerry Pate standing on dry land! Pate has a habit of doing Mark Spitz impersonations . . When he won the 1981 Memphis Classic he dived into a lake next to the 18th green. He also went for a dip when he won the Tournament Players' Championship in 1982, but this time he took US Tour Commissioner Deane Beman with him

When he wins a tournament, Jerry Pate certainly turns it into a dramatic and memorable occasion. When he won the 1981 Danny Thomas-Memphis Classic he celebrated his first Tour win for three years by diving fully clothed into the lake by the 18th green. The picture of him making his splash was seen in newspapers the world over. After winning the Tournament Players' Championship at Sawgrass in Florida the following year he repeated his aquatic feat but not until he had pushed Tour Commissioner Deane Beman and course architect Pete Dye into the lake first.

'Jack was heavier than I am.'

When likened to Jack Nicklaus, who also won the US Open in his Rookie year

---

An outstanding amateur

Conrad Rehling, the man who developed Bob Murphy in the 1960s, discovered Pate while coaching at a college near Pate's home in Pensacola, Florida. Pate was still at school at the time but when Rehling moved to the University of Alabama Pate followed.

He had a great amateur career and in 1974, the year before turning professional, he won the Florida Amateur title, was a member of the US team that won the World Amateur Team Championship and won the US Amateur title beating John Grace 2 & 1 at Ridgewood, New Jersey. It was the first time Pate had qualified for the championship.

To follow his professional career

As well as being a good swimmer Jerry Pate is a pretty useful golfer, as his fine record shows

Pate borrowed $4,000 from Crawford Drainwater, a family friend. Jerry's father, a Coca-Cola distributor, would have loaned him the money but he insisted on borrowing from outside the family. That way he knew he would have to pay it back, and to pay it back he would have to win. And that is what Jerry Pate set about doing.

From top amateur to top rookie

His professional career continued where his amateur career left off. He won a record $153,102 by a Rookie and was tenth on the 1976 money-list. It was winning his first Tour event, the US Open, however, which really brought him to everyone's attention.

Playing at the Atlanta Athletic Club in Georgia Pate won the title with a brilliant five-iron at the 72nd hole which was played across water and within 2 feet (60 cm) of the pin for a birdie putt and the championship. He won the title on Father's Day and he gave the gold watch, which was part of his prize, to his father.

Youngest US Open champion since Nicklaus

At 22 he became the youngest US Open champion since Jack Nicklaus in 1962. Coincidentally, Nicklaus' first Tour win was also the US Open and naturally comparisons between Pate and the great man were being made. Those comparisons were heightened a few weeks later when Jerry won the Canadian Open, often regarded as the fifth major. He beat Nicklaus by four strokes and his final round of 63 was a championship record.

Wins in the Southern Open and Phoenix Open the following year, and a Southern Open repeat in 1978 established Pate as a leading money-winner. Although he went without a win until the 1981 Danny Thomas, he was still a top-ten finisher and between 1978 and 1982 never finished lower than tenth on the money-list. His win in the Danny Thomas took his total career earnings over $1 million and at 27 he was the youngest person to reach that milestone.

Sudden decline

A dramatic decline in his game set in midway through the 1982 season when a neck muscle injury threatened his career. Despite tests

over the next couple of years it was not until the spring of 1985 that the trouble was diagnosed as a torn cartilage in his left shoulder. By then Pate had slumped to 188th on the money-list and won a mere $7,000 in 1985. Operations in 1985 and 1986 meant he missed most of the season. Sadly the problem did not appear to have been overcome in 1987 when he entered only a handful of US Tour events. If that injury which has threatened a brilliant career clears up soon Jerry Pate should return to his former glories. He is only in his early thirties and the golf world could expect more dramatics from Pate.

LEADING TOURNAMENT WINS

1976
US Open
Canadian Open

1982
Tournament Players' Championship

COREY PAVIN

Born: 16 November 1959, Oxnard, California, USA
Height: 5 ft 9 in (1.75 m)
Weight: 140 lb (63.5 kg)
Turned professional: 1981
First US Tour win: 1984 Houston Coca-Cola open

Since 1984 Corey Pavin has been a regular winner on the US Tour

There can be few men who can claim victories in each of their first four years on the US Tour. Only great men like Jack Nicklaus have had such an impressive start to their careers. Perhaps in Corey Pavin another great career is emerging because he has been a winner every year since he joined the Tour in 1984.

An exceptional junior

His outstanding career as a junior started in 1977 when he won the World Junior title and at 17 became the youngest winner of the Los Angeles amateur title. He followed that with 11 wins at UCLA, a Walker Cup appearance, and in 1982 he won the Fred Haskins Award as the year's outstanding collegiate player. Until his late teens Corey weighed less than 100 lb (45.36 kg) which helped to develop his game. When other players were taking a wedge he was still getting in practice with a 3-iron!

A shaky professional debut

Pavin turned professional in 1981 but failed to come through the qualifying school at the first attempt. He played in other parts of the world for experience and won the South African and German Opens, as well as the Calberson Classic in France. When he returned to the USA in late 1983 he had no difficulty in coming through the Tour school.

He missed the cut in his first Tour event, the 1984 Bob Hope Classic, but in the second pushed Tom Purtzer all the way at Phoenix in Arizona before Purtzer won with a birdie at the 72nd. Pavin won the Houston Coca-Cola Open in his Rookie year and his earnings of $260,536 were the highest by a first-year player in the history of the Tour, beating the $237,000 of Hal Sutton two years earlier.

LEADING TOURNAMENT WINS

1984
Houston Coca-Cola Open

1985
Colonial National Invitation

1986
Hawaiian Open
Greater Milwaukee Open

1987
Bob Hope Desert Classic
Hawaiian Open

Success, success and more success

Pavin has an excellent swing, and credit for that, and all aspects of his game, goes to Bruce Hamilton, the professional at Las Posas Country Club in Camirillo, California. He has worked with Pavin since 1975.

As a second-year professional Pavin finished the season sixth on the money list and in 1986 collected more than $300,000 for a second consecutive season. It was an eventful year for Corey and wife Shannon because their first son, Ryan, arrived mid-way through the season.

The Corey Pavin success story continued in 1987 as he won the Bob Hope Classic and Hawaiian Open within three weeks of each other as he took his career earnings well past $1 million with seasons winings of nearly $500,000.

US Tour's Rookie of the Year

Corey Pavin has joined some illustrious names in recent years winning this award.
1976 Jerry Pate
1977 Graham Marsh
1978 Pat McGowan
1979 John Fought
1980 Gary Halberg
1981 Mark O'Meara
1982 Hal Sutton
1983 Nick Price
1984 Corey Pavin
1985 Phil Blackmar
1986 Davis Love III
1987 Keith Clearwater

STYLE POINTS

Has a nice fluent swing and is a very accurate shot-maker.

CALVIN PEETE

Born: 18 July 1943, Detroit, Michigan, USA

Height: 5 ft 10 in (1.78 m)

Weight: 165 lb (74.8 kg)

Turned professional: 1971

First US Tour win: 1979 Greater Milwaukee Open

For one of the game's most consistent performers with the driver, you need to look no further than Calvin Peete. Every year since 1981 he has topped the US Tour driving accuracy statistics, regularly hitting the target with 80 per cent of his drives. It is consistency like that which has helped make Calvin Peete one of the top money-winners in the 1980s.

'Who wants to chase a little ball around under the hot sun?'

To his friends who were regularly trying to get him to join them for a game of golf

'. . . I'd be happy making a third of that chasing that ball.'

After he found out Jack Nicklaus earned $200,000 a year for playing golf!

A slow professional start

Although a professional since 1971 it took him four years before he came through the qualifying school. He joined the US Tour in 1976 and won his first tournament, the Greater Milwaukee Open in 1979, and finished 27th on the money-list. His next success was in 1982 and since then he has been a regular winner on the Tour, with the exception of 1987 when he finished outside the top 50 for the first time for ten years.

Calvin won four tournaments in 1982 and was fourth on the money-list, a position he held the follow-

'King' Calvin . . . after winning the 1986 Tournament of Champions

ing year. He was the Vardon trophy winner in 1984 and in 1985 enjoyed his best season with earnings of $384,489, a sum that took him to third in the money-list. Victory in the Tournament Players' Championship considerably swelled his winnings; it also meant he was exempt from qualifying for US Tour events for the next ten years. Peete took his career earnings past $2 million in 1986.

Handicap no handicap

He won the 1983 golf writers' Ben Hogan Award for golfers who have had to overcome a handicap. Calvin broke his left elbow as a youngster and cannot straighten his arm properly. His accuracy and success therefore defy golf's theory that you should keep a straight left arm.

A very late starter

Peete was brought up on a Florida farm with his 18 brothers and sisters from his father's two marriages. To earn much-needed money for the family, Peete had to leave school early. A job as a travelling salesman selling household goods took him to Rochester, New Jersey, were he made some friends who were constantly trying to persuade him to join them for a game of golf. After regularly turning them down, because the game did not appeal to him, he eventually agreed. That was in 1966, when he was 23 and he soon got hooked on the game. At the same time he watched Jack Nicklaus on television, and when he heard the Golden Bear earned around $200,000 a year he thought he'd like to play golf professionally.

Completely self taught, he used to watch Gene Littler playing in his early days and pick up pointers. It was five years before he turned professional and the rest of Calvin Peete's career speaks for itself in his impressive list of achievements.

LEADING TOURNAMENT WINS

1979
Greater Milwaukee Open

1982
Greater Milwaukee Open
Anheuser–Busch Classic
BC Open
Pensacoloa Open

1983
Atlanta Classic
Anheuser-Busch Classic

1984
Texas Open

1985
Phoenix Open
Tournament Players'
Championship

1986
Tournament of Champions
USF & G Classic

STYLE POINTS

Can't bend his left elbow and has a looping swing.

MANUEL PINERO

Born: 1 September 1952, Badajoz, Spain
Height: 5 ft 7 in (1.7 m)
Weight: 143 lb (64.9 kg)
Turned professional: 1968
First European Tour win: 1974 Madrid Open

One of the stars of the Europeans' Ryder Cup win over the United States 12 months earlier, Spain's Manuel Pinero had his worst season on the European Tour for 13 years in 1986 when he slipped to 32nd place, and with no better than a fifth placing from the 18 tournaments played.

Putting problem

Being fairly short Pinero lacks the power of many of his fellow professionals, but his short game is second to none. However, his major problem in 1986 was with his putter. He has never been totally comfortable on the putting surface. He used to tremble at the thought of putting at one time but he got over it. The fear returned in 1986. He changed his putter, and then changed the replacement and kept changing them, putter after putter but he still couldn't get it right. In the end he decided to stick with one and try hard to get used to it, but by then it was too late to salvage anything from the season.

His season reached a complete low when he was disqualified from the Dunhill Masters after television viewers phoned to say he had taken an unfair advantage when playing out of the rough. He was fined £1,000 but his integrity was not questioned by the PGA.

Rags to riches

Pinero's rise to become one of the leading European golfers is a classic rags to riches tale.

His pig farming family moved to Madrid when Manuel was 11. He was educated at a caddie school where he received a basic education, but more important, he earned money caddying and also learned how to play golf. Current professionals Jose-Maria Canizares and Antonio Garrido were fellow members of the school.

Pinero turned professional at 16 and won his first Tour event six years later when he beat Valentin Barrios in a play-off to win the Madrid Open.

Pinero has twice enjoyed success in the World Cup as a member of the winning Spanish team, in 1976 with Severiano Ballesteros and in 1982 with Canizares, when Pinero also took the individual title. In team play his greatest moment was in the Ryder Cup at the Belfry course near Birmingham in 1985.

First selected for the Ryder Cup in 1981, he missed out two years later but in 1985 he played an important part in the first European victory over the USA for 28 years and his 3 & 1 win over Lanny Wadkins in the opening singles was the platform the European team needed to build on.

To crown a memorable year for Manuel, his first child, Laura, was born to him and wife Angeles. It is to be hoped that the memories and glories of his golfing successes in 1985 will soon be re-captured.

Spain's Manuel Pinero (left) with his Ryder Cup captain Tony Jacklin at the Belfry in 1985. Pinero played his part in the first defeat of the Americans for 28 years

LEADING TOURNAMENT WINS

1974
Madrid Open

1976
Swiss Open

1977
PGA Championship

1981
Madrid Open
Swiss Open

1982
European Open

1985
Madrid Open
Italian Open

GARY PLAYER

Born: 1 November 1935, Johannesburg, South Africa	
Height: 5 ft 7 in (1.7 m)	
Weight: 150 lb (68 kg)	
Turned professional: 1953	
First professional win: 1955 Egyptian Match-Play Championship	

Take a look at Gary Player's waistline and then compare it against a picture of him 25 years ago. Can you spot the difference? Well, to be honest you are not likely to because there isn't any. A keep-fit fanatic and strict dieter, Player is a great believer in physical fitness being the key to a successful life – and in his case, a successful golf career as well. Totally dedicated, he still spends hours practising even though he has reached the top of his profession. His game is now centred upon the popular US Seniors Tour, which he joined on reaching his 50th birthday in 1985. Since joining the Tour he has continued winning where he left off. Gary can still pack power into those drives of his, but he will best be remembered for his magnificent bunker-play which, over the years, has saved him strokes and won him tournaments.

The epitome of a great sportsman, his father was a Johannesburg mining official who became a widower when Gary was eight. Player turned professional in 1953 when he was 17 and only four years after his father first persuaded him to take up the game. Gary became assistant to Jock Verwey and in 1955 won his first tournament as a professional, the Egyptian Match-Play title at Cairo's Geziva Club, beating fellow South African Harold Henning in the final.

He headed for England the following year and won the Dunlop tournament at Sunningdale in Berkshire. Britain was a stopping-off point for the United States where he made his debut in 1957.

Gary Player teeing off at the first tee at Cherry Hills in 1985

Playing the Americans at their own game

Over the next 21 years he won 21 US Tour events, starting with the 1958 Kentucky Derby Open. If he had played the US Tour regularly, instead of jetting across the world to play in other countries, and also returning to his native Johannesburg where he firmly maintained his roots, there is no knowing what an impact he would have had in the United States.

Player was the first non-US golfer to attack the Americans seriously and he did it successfully, winning nearly $2 million and taking all three American major titles. He won nine major championships during his career, starting in 1959 when he won the Open in Britain over Muirfield's rugged 6,800-yard (6,216-metre) layout, pulling back an eight-shot deficit on Frank Bullock over the last 36 holes. His last major win was in the US Masters 19 years later. His nine wins is the joint fourth best of all time and the man he shares that distinction with is Ben Hogan, the player who Gary modelled himself on in his early days. Hogan, Player, Jack Nicklaus and Gene Sarazen are the only men to have won all four professional major championships.

The big three

For three decades Gary Player showed himself as a tough competitor and in the 1960s with Arnold Palmer and Jack Nicklaus was one of the so-called Big Three managed by Mark McCormack. Their impact on golf, not only in dominating the major events, but in exhibition play had a lasting effect on the sport. Their attitude and skills were instrumental in many people taking up the sport.

As for Player, he has won golf tournaments all over the world including his own South African Open a record 13 times. He has won the Australian Open seven times and when he won the title in 1974 it was the 100th win of his career. By late 1987 he had won over 130 tournaments.

Match-play expert

If there was one tournament Gary made his own it was the World Match-Play Championship at Wentworth in Surrey. In the ten years between 1965 and 1974 he appeared in six finals, winning five. Only Hale Irwin in 1974 beat him in the final. During that time he was involved in some great matches. There was the 1973 final when Australian Graham Marsh took Player to the 40th hole before

STYLE POINTS

Stands a long way from the ball at address. Few better at bunker play. Keeps his head low over the ball when putting.

succumbing. The greatest match in the history of the competition, and one of match-play's all-time great confrontations, was in 1965 when he beat Tony Lema at the 37th hole. Trailing by seven holes with 17 to play Player produced one of the sport's greatest comebacks to win the 36th hole and

---

'I'm glad we didn't have a play-off. I'm scared of sudden-death play-offs. I've lost 17 of them!'

About the 1978 US Masters

'It's truly amazing, the more I practise the luckier I get!'

During the 1981 British Open in reply to a shout of 'You lucky little South African'.

Gary Player and Arnold Palmer (watching) during the 1964 World Match-Play Championship

halve the match before winning at the first extra hole.

Memorable moments are plentiful in the career of Gary Player. But winning the 1978 US Masters at the age of 42 and 17 years after first winning the title gave him as much pleasure as any of his other great wins because he came from seven behind leader Hubert Green on the final day to win one of the closest Masters for years by a single stroke, thanks to seven birdies in the last 10 holes. At the start of the final round he wasn't even considered a potential victor.

Gary was ninth on the US money-list in 1978, and was still showing many up-and-coming youngsters a thing or two about the great game. That was his last winning season in the United States until he started taking the Seniors Tour by storm in 1985.

Family man

Like his father, Gary runs a farm in Johannesburg and has firmly maintained his roots in his homeland. He regards his family life as important as his golf. He is married to Vivien Verwey, the daughter of Gary's first mentor, and they have six children – four of them were born in years when Gary won a major. One of his sons, 25-year-old Wayne, is following in his father's footsteps and could well carry on the family name within the golfing world.

LEADING TOURNAMENT WINS

1959
British Open

1961
US Masters

1962
US PGA Championship

1965
US Open
World Match-Play Championship
World Cup (team and individual)

1966
World Match-Play Championship

1968
British Open
World Match-Play Championship

1971
World Match-Play Championship

1972
US PGA Championship

1973
World Match-Play Championship

1974
US Masters
British Open

1977
World Cup (individual)

1978
US Masters

DAN POHL

Born: 1 April 1955, Mount Pleasant, Michigan, USA	
Height: 5 ft 11 in (1.8 m)	
Weight: 175 lb (79.4 kg)	
Turned professional: 1977	
First US Tour win: 1986 Colonial National Invitation	

Dan Pohl finally did in 1986 what he had been threatening for seven years: win a tournament. He had nearly done so many times since he joined the Tour in 1978, and five times had won over $90,000 in a season, without recording a win. Since then Pohl has been one of the big money-winners on the Tour, winning more than $900,000 in the two seasons 1986 and 1987 alone.

He started playing golf at the age of five but baseball and basketball were his first loves.

LEADING TOURNAMENT WINS

1986
Colonial National Invitation
NEC World Series of Golf

A debt to baseball
When he went to Arizona he took his powerful baseball swing with him and today he is one of the biggest hitters on the US Tour.

He won the Michigan State Amateur title in 1975 and 1977 and turned professional in the second of those years. He qualified through the Tour school in the

---

'Dan Pohl did what he had to do to succeed . . . relax.'

Explaining how he eventually made the breakthrough and had his first wins on the US Tour

---

spring of 1978 but had such a bad first year he had to re-qualify in 1979. In that second year he attracted a lot of attention when he led the Western Open with three to play but as he said: 'I got all pumped up', and he bogeyed the last three to finish a tie for third place.

Pohl had a habit of trying to force the play when getting in a winning position and it was that characteristic that possibly cost him a chance of the 1982 US Masters when he lost a play-off to Craig Stadler.

Pohl finally got it all right in 1986 and steadied himself to win those first tournaments that had been promising for so long. He beat Payne Stewart on the first extra hole to win the Colonial National Invitation and three months later he won the World Series at Akron, Ohio. Although without a win in 1987 he won $465,000 and was selected for the Ryder Cup team for the first time.

Dan Pohl, one of the rising stars of US golf and the 1987 Vardon Trophy winner

NICK PRICE

Born: 28 January 1957, Durban, South Africa

Height: 6 ft (1.83 m)

Weight: 175 lb (79.4 kg)

Turned professional: 1977

First major professional win: 1979 Asseng Invitational (South Africa)

When he was 17 Nick Price was invited to play in the Junior World tournament at Torrey Pines in California. He returned home as champion.

Price started playing golf at the age of eight shortly after caddying for his brother. He played on the South African and European Tours as an amateur in 1975 but then joined the Rhodesian Air Force for two years. He came out just in time to join the South African Tour, but this time as a professional.

> **'I can't believe it was that easy to win.'**
>
> *After winning his first US Tour event*

British disaster

His game really took off in 1980 when he won the Swiss Open and followed it with the South African Masters the next year. In 1982 he had the biggest disappointment of his career when he led the British Open at Troon in Scotland by three strokes with six to play but dropped four shots over those last six holes and let Tom Watson in to beat him by one.

American success

All that was forgotten in 1983 when he won the World Series of Golf in Ohio, beating Jack Nicklaus by four strokes. It gained Price exemption from prequalifying for US Tour events for ten years, and he has been a regular on the Tour ever since.

Nick Price now has his home in Orlando, Florida, and when he is not playing golf there is a good chance you will see him playing tennis, or fishing, or engaging in one of the many water sports he enjoys . . . all with the same determination as he plays his golf.

South Africa's Nick Price during the 1986 US Masters at Augusta. He created history by shooting a third-round 63, a new championship record

JOSE RIVERO

Born: 20 September 1955, Madrid, Spain	
Height: 5 ft 8 in (1.73 m)	
Weight: 148 lb (67.1 kg)	
Turned professional: 1973	
First European Tour win: 1984 Lawrence Batley International	

Two of the finest moments in the career of Spain's Jose Rivero were both at the beautiful English Belfry course near Birmingham. It was the scene of Rivero's first European Tour win in 1984 when he holed a 10-foot (3-metre) putt under pressure to win the Lawrence Batley International, and the following year he was in the European team that wrested the Ryder Cup from the Americans after 28 years.

Batley. Jacklin felt they were ideal for such a situation. Pinero, a brilliant short game player, and his partner did not disappoint their skipper and they soundly beat the strong US pairing of Tom Kite and Calvin Peete 7 & 5 to help Europe to a healthy position for the final day.

It may have appeared to some that Rivero was an overnight success but he had been a professional since 1973. However, he did not become a tournament professional until 1984, preferring to spend more time at his Madrid club. The Spanish Golf Federation loaned him £2,500 towards the expenses of playing on the Tour but £60,000 winnings in his first full season enabled him to repay the money and become self sufficient.

Winless since 1984, Jose came third to Sandy Lyle in the 1985 Open in Britain but returned to the winner's rostrum in 1987 when he won the French Open at St Cloud in Paris thanks to ten birdies and a record-equalling 63 in the final round to win by one from Howard Clark. His winnings of £41,000 set him well on his way to topping the £100,000-mark for the season, which assured him a second Ryder Cup place in 1987, and a second appearance on the wining side.

Jose Rivero, one of four Spaniards who helped win the Ryder Cup at the Belfry in 1985

'Since I've lived in Spain I've seen a lot of this man and I like what I've seen.'

Ryder Cup captain Tony Jacklin

Ryder Cup glory

With the pressure on, captain Tony Jacklin, who selected Rivero as one of his three personal choices, threw Rivero and his partner Canizares into a vital match. The two of them had a year earlier won the World Cup for Spain, and Jacklin was impressed with the way Rivero holed his putt to win the Lawrence

LEADING TOURNAMENT WINS

1984
*Lawrence Batley International
World Cup (with Jose-Maria Canizares)*

1987
French Open

STYLE POINTS

Has a mechanical putting stroke which comes from the shoulders. When driving or playing from the fairway has a nice follow-through.

PETER SENIOR

Born: 31 July 1959, Singapore

Height: 5 ft 5 in (1.65 m)

Weight: 163 lb (73.9 kg)

Turned professional: 1978

First major professional win: 1979 South Australian Open

In 1987 Peter Senior established himself as one of the big names of European golf and finished in the top ten in the Order of Merit with winnings of over £100,000. But of course he had to give a share of that to his caddie . . . wife June!

American failure, European success

A few months on the US Tour early in 1986 cost Peter Senior and his wife June, his regular caddie, around $30,000, yet his prize money was a mere $2,500 in 12 outings. With his confidence gone, he left the Tour and headed for the European Tour. By the end of the season he had his US expenditure, and a bit more, duly returned.

Success in the new PLM Open in Sweden and a share of third place in the Monte Carlo Open took his earnings to £40,000, more than his total on his three previous exploits on the European Tour.

He tried his luck on the European Tour for the first time in 1979. He returned in 1984 and has been a regular ever since but his first win was not until that PLM Open at Malmo when he beat Swedes Mats Lanner and Ove Sellberg into second and third places.

A great run of success followed in 1987 when Peter won the fog-bound Monte Carlo Open in record-breaking style. He held off a challenge from fellow Australian Rodger Davis to win by one shot with a Tour record equalling 260 and 14-under par. Coincidentally, the record of 260 was previously held by two other Australians, Kel Nagle and Mike Clayton.

A rising Australian star of the 1980s, Peter Senior, seeking advice from his caddie at St Pierre, Chepstow

LEADING TOURNAMENT WINS

1979
South Australian Open

1984
Queensland Open
New South Wales PGA

1986
PLM Open

1987
New South Wales PGA
Monte Carlo Open

SCOTT SIMPSON

Born:	17 September 1955, San Diego, California, USA
Height:	6 ft 2 in (1.88 m)
Weight:	180 lb (81.7 kg)
Turned professional:	1977
First US Tour win:	1980 Western Open

When Scott Simpson won the 1987 US Open at the Olympic Club, San Francisco, it was further proof that a small elite band of players no longer had a monopoly on the world's major championships. Simpson was the 16th different winner of 16 consecutive majors. Runner-up Tom

> **'There will be days when others beat him, but there will not be many when Simpson beats himself.'**
>
> *Jack Nicklaus about Scott Simpson*

Watson was not the slightest bit surprised to see Scott take the title. He had been watching Simpson for some time and acknowledged him as a very steady player.

Born in San Diego, Scott still lives there but plays out of the Makaha Valley Club, Hawaii.

His first involvement with golf was at the age of nine when he used to caddy for his scratch-handicap father. He played in his first tournament when he was ten and tied in fifth place.

Great amateur career

He became a successful college player and left the amateur game with a great record behind him. He was runner-up in the US Junior championship, was twice the NCAA Champion, and the winner of the California and San Diego junior titles, among others. It was after winning his first NCAA title

that Scott knew he could make it as a professional. He felt that if he could win from a field containing the best college players, there was every chance he could make the grade as a pro. Shortly after a successful Walker Cup appearance in 1977 he made the transition, but it was only at the third attempt, that he made it through the Tour qualifying school.

Apart from his Rookie season Scott has finished in the top 50 every season and was one of the top money-winners in 1987 thanks to victories in the Greensboro Open and the US Open, when he played the best putting round in his life to finish with a 68 and beat Watson by one shot. He added to his Walker Cup honours with selection for the 1987 US Ryder Cup team that

played Europe at the Muirfield Village course in Ohio.

Scott Simpson just quietly gets on with his game and lets his golf do the talking. He has always believed his golf could get better, and hard work is the key. He has borne that out having emerged as one of the biggest money-winners on the US Tour since 1985. The name of Scott Simpson will never again be a surprise when being engraved on a major championship trophy.

A kiss from wife Cheryl says it all after Scott Simpson had won his first major, the 1987 US Open at the Olympic Club in 1987

LEADING TOURNAMENT WINS

1980
Western Open

1984
Manufacturers Hanover-Westchester Classic

1987
*Greater Greensboro Open
US Open*

STYLE POINTS

Outstanding bunker player.

J. C. SNEAD

Born:	14 October 1941, Hot Springs, Virginia, USA
Height:	6 ft 2 in (1.88 m)
Weight:	200 lb (90.7 kg)
Turned professional:	1964
First US Tour win:	1971 Tucson Open

Although originally known as the nephew of the legendary Sam Snead, Jesse Carlyle Snead (known as J.C.)'s golfing record since the late 1960s stands in its own right.

A superb athlete in his teens, he had set his heart on being a baseball player and was in the Washington Senators junior squad but suddenly turned to golf and eventually got a job with Charlie Beverage, the professional at the Century Country Club in Westchester County. He spent four years trying to get his Tour card, which he obtained in 1968.

After three years learning the ropes on the Tour, J.C. burst on to the scene in 1971 with wins in the Tucson and Doral-Eastern Opens. He finished 17th on the money-list

One of the game's most popular guys, J. C. Snead. Much sought after as a tutor of the game, he has carried on the Snead tradition instituted by his uncle, the great Sam Snead, just before the Second World War. Sam won a record 84 Tour events

---

'Jessie Carlyle hasn't been playing worth a damn.'

His reason for reverting to being called JC: a lean period followed his decision to use his full name

---

and appeared in the first of three consecutive Ryder Cup matches. Throughout the 1970s he remained in the top 50 and twice came close to a major. He lost by one shot to Tommy Aaron in the 1973 US Masters after leading with nine to play, before putting his ball into Rae's Creek alongside the 12th. At Cherry Hills in Denver, Colorado, in 1978 he lost by one shot again, this time to Andy North in the US Open. Shortly afterwards he broke a bone in his wrist and missed seven weeks of the Tour.

1987 revival

After winning two tournaments and a personal best $192,645 in the 1976 season Snead went five years before his next Tour win, the 1981 Southern Open. After that it was another six years before he had win number eight when he was well in control to beat Seve Ballesteros at the first extra hole to win the Westchester Classic. At 46 he enjoyed a new lease of life and took his season's earnings past the $200,000 mark for the first time in his career as total earnings soared towards $2 million.

As he approaches his Seniors golfing days, he devotes a lot of time to helping youngsters develop their game and gives his time willingly – that is assuming it doesn't interfere, with his favourite pastime, big game hunting!

Snead, one of the game's great shot maker's, is gaining a reputation as one of the game's great teachers as well. In addition to lending his time to helping youngsters, many fellow professionals call on him for advice and he gives it willingly.

LEADING TOURNAMENT WINS

1971
Tucson Open
Doral-Eastern Open

1972
Philadelphia Classic

1975
Andy Williams–San Diego Open

1976
Andy Williams–San Diego Open
Kaiser International

1981
Southern Open

1987
Westchester Classic

HOLLIS STACY

Born: 16 March 1954, Savannah, Georgia, USA

Height: 5 ft 5 in (1.65 m)

Weight: 133 lb (60.3 kg)

Turned professional: 1974

First US LPGA Tour win: 1977 Rail Charity Golf Classic

When Hollis Stacy became the fifth woman to win a third US Open title in 1984 it was her 16th US LPGA Tour win, but her first for 11 months. The winless run ended at the Salem Country Club, Massachusetts, when she beat Rosie Jones by a single stroke. The victory was sealed at the 341-yard (312-metre) dog-leg 13th when she played what was described as the golf shot of the year, when she played a remarkable seven-iron second shot that went into the hole for an eagle two.

three times. When she won in 1969 at 15 years 4 months old she was the youngest ever winner of the title.

Stacy turned professional in 1974 but did not have her first win until 1977. She set the US LPGA Tour alight that year. In winning her first tournament the Rail Charity Classic at Springfield, Illinois, her winning total of 271 shattered the Tour record. She then added the Lady Tara Classic

and US Open championship, leading from start to finish. She retained the US Open the following year.

When Hollis won her third title in 1984 her mother ordered a case of champagne for the press tent, reminiscent of Tony Lema's antics 20 years earlier.

Three times winner of the US Women's Open, Hollis Stacy. She won the US Women's Open two years' running in 1977 and 1978

LEADING TOURNAMENT WINS

1977
US Women's Open

1978
US Women's Open

1983
Peter Jackson Classic

1984
US Women's Open

Junior prodigy

One of ten children, Hollis started playing golf at the age of 11 and took to it instantly. Guidance and help came from her mother Tillie, a keen golfer and member of the US Golf Association's Women's Committee. It was not long before Hollis was winning titles and she was the three-times winner of the US Junior title between 1969 and 1971 – the only person to win it

CRAIG STADLER

Born: 2 June 1953, San Diego, California, USA
Height: 5 ft 10 in (1.78 m)
Weight: 200 lb (90.7 kg)
Turned professional: 1975
First US Tour win: 1980 Bob Hope Desert Classic

As an amateur Craig Stadler was coached at the University of Southern California by Stan Wood, who says that Stadler was one of the three best golfers he coached in 25 years. The others were Al Geiberger and Dave Stockton.

Stadler left the amateur game with a fine record. He was the World Junior champion in 1971 and went on to win the US Amateur championship at Inverness in Ohio in 1973 when he beat David Strawn 6 & 5 in the first championship for nine years to be played under match-play conditions. His amateur days were completed with Walker Cup honours. Shortly afterwards he turned professional, in 1975.

Although he had great natural ability his biggest problem was controlling his temper. He worked hard on both his game and his emotions and eventually got it right. But the going was not easy for Stadler in his early days on the Tour, which he joined after coming through the school in the autumn of 1976. He showed signs that he was a good player and in 1980 had his first win, in the Bob Hope Desert Classic. He followed that with the Greater Greensboro Open and in 1981 won the Kemper Open to give him winnings of $200,000 for the second successive season. It was in 1982 that Craig Stadler emerged as a great player.

> **'I wish they would talk about my golf and not my wardrobe: print my score – not my measurements.'**
>
> *About the press, who were more intent on covering his rotund waistline than his golf play*

One of the game's most colourful characters 'The Walrus' . . . alias Craig Stadler

A truly great year

He won four tournaments including the US Masters and World Series of Golf, and was the top money-winner with over $440,000. However, he nearly threw away his one and only major when bogeys at the 12th, 14th, 16th and 18th holes in the US Masters lost him a six-stroke lead and he had to endure a play-off against Dan Pohl, playing his first Masters, before winning the sudden-death at the first extra hole. Craig Stadler became the first Masters winner to wear a size 48 champion's green jacket! Another play-off was needed to beat Ray Floyd in the end-of-season World Series of Golf at Akron, and a memorable season was crowned with wife Sue presenting him with their second son, Christopher.

Although Stadler has not had a season like that since he has remained a consistent money-winner, apart from a slight hiccup in 1986 when he slipped to 53rd on the money-list. He has won eight Tour events and over $2,250,000 in his 12 years as a professional.

A very frustrated Craig Stadler during the 1987 British Open at Muirfield. In contention after two opening 69s he finished tied eighth

LEADING TOURNAMENT WINS

1980
Bob Hope Desert Classic
Greater Greensboro Open

1981
Kemper Open

1982
US Masters
World Series of Golf
Joe Garagiola–Tucson Open
Kemper Open

1984
Byron Nelson Classic

A great favourite with galleries the world over, he is nicknamed the Walrus because of his rotund figure and large walrus-type moustache. Among his hobbies away from the golf course he enjoys playing the stock market, skiing and hunting. He is also a great fan of the San Diego Padres baseball team.

The game of golf can recall many great moments. It can also recall many cruel and tragic moments. Craig Stadler has certainly played his part in the latter. It was during the 1985 Ryder Cup at the Belfry, Sutton Coldfield, near Birmingham. Playing for the USA with Curtis Strange in the second morning's foursomes against Europe's Sandy Lyle and Bernhard Langer, Craig had a 2-foot (60-cm) putt to halve the hole and win the last match of the morning. He missed and the halved match resulted in the scores being level at six-all. The miss demoralized Stadler and sent the spirits of the European team sky-high and they went on to register their first win since 1957.

Happily the career of Craig Stadler has not been one of constant disappointments like that. On the contrary: he has been one of America's most successful and popular golfers of the 1980s.

JAN STEPHENSON

Born: 22 December 1951, Sydney, Australia	
Height: 5 ft 5 in (1.65 m)	
Weight: 117 lb (53.1 kg)	
Turned professional: 1973	
First US Tour win: 1976 Sarah Coventry Naples Classic	

Jan Stephenson's biggest problem on the US Tour has been her devastating good looks. Her early days on the Tour were spent fending off the offers from *Playboy* and *Penthouse* who wanted her to model for them. But take a close look at Jan Stephenson, she can also play golf . . .

Outstanding as a junior, Jan Stephenson won a New South Wales title every year from 1964 to 1972, as a schoolgirl, junior and senior. She turned professional in 1973 and immediately headed for the United States where she was Rookie of the Year in 1974, finishing 28th on the money-list. She has since been one of the top money-winners, without ever topping the list, and by late 1987 had surpassed the $1 million mark in career winnings.

Jan set a Tour record in 1981 when she broke the 54-hole record during the Mary Kay Classic at Bent Tree in Dallas, Texas. Her rounds of 65, 69 and 64 for a total of 198 beat the old record by two strokes.

'Maybe people will stop thinking of me only as a sex symbol and realize I can really play golf.'

After winning the 1983 US Open

American honours

The greatest moment of Jan's career was in 1983 when she beat the Americans JoAnne Carner and Patty Sheehan to win the US Open, and become the third non-American after Catherine Lacoste of France and Fay Crocker of Uruguay to win the title. Her victory was completed in 100°F (38° C) heat and it was her eighth Tour win in two years. She had started the 1983 season with the remarkable record of playing in more than 175 tournaments without missing the cut.

In 1982 Jan married Ernie Vossler and they spend their relaxation hours flying their own plane. Jan is also the honorary chairman of the National Multiple Sclerosis Society and a golf course designer, the first woman professional golfer ever to take to course design.

Australia's Jan Stephenson could have earned money as a model but resisted some lucrative offers to carry on playing golf

LEADING TOURNAMENT WINS

1973
Australian Open

1977
Australian Open

1981
Peter Jackson Classic

1982
US LPGA Championship

1983
US Women's Open

PAYNE STEWART

Born: 30 January 1957, Springfield, Missouri, USA	
Height: 6 ft 1 in (1.85 m)	
Weight: 175 lb (79.4 kg)	
Turned professional: 1979	
First US Tour win: 1982 Quad Cities Open	

Between winning the 1983 Walt Disney Classic and the Hertz Bay Hill Classic four years later, Payne Stewart found himself in a position to add to his number of wins many times, but could not inflict that last killer blow to take the title. Consider his record during that period. He played in 94 tournaments, had 32 top ten finishes, was runner-up nine times, and lost three play-offs. If he had converted half those second placings to wins he would have topped the money-list on a couple of occasions.

A man of weaker character could well have crumbled under such frustration but Payne, encouraged by his Australian wife Tracey, carried on, and with greater determination than ever.

A winner at $4\frac{1}{2}$

Stewart first picked up a golf club at the age of four and was encouraged by his father Bill, who was a keen golfer. At the age of four and a half Payne won his first tournament, a local father and son competition over three holes! Bill was a good golfer and twice won the Missouri State Amateur championship, a championship his son was also to win.

Payne turned professional in 1979 after a successful amateur career that saw him win the Southwest Conference, All-America and Missouri Amateur titles, and all in his last year as an amateur. He had to wait until the spring of 1981 before coming through the Tour qualifying school. He made little impact on the Tour in his first year, but had a successful time playing the Asian Tour, finishing third on their Order of Merit.

Payne Stewart seen here in action during the 1986 Open at Turnberry

He made his breakthrough in 1982 by winning the Quad Cities tournament and ended the season a commendable 38th on the money-list. Since then he has not figured outside the top 20.

His winnings of $535,389 in 1986 were a Tour record by a player not winning during the season, but his catalogue of near-misses still haunted him, and there was not a more painful reminder than in the US Open. Having finished second to Sandy Lyle in the Open at Sandwich in Kent in 1985 it looked at Shinnecock Hills on Long Island as if he was going to win a major championship. The third-round leader, Greg Norman, had fallen by the wayside and at the 13th Payne was in the lead but it soon disappeared as Ray Floyd, the eventual winner, Lanny Wadkins and Chip Back sailed past him on their way to shooting scores in the mid-60s, while Stewart could do no better than a final-round 70.

After that disappointment Stewart was on the verge of packing the game in, or at least giving it a rest. But wife Tracey encouraged him to carry on and, more important, she made him go and see Harvie Ward, the pro at Interlachen. Ward, as an amateur, was many times fancied for big events, but could never quite pull it off. He gave sound advice and encouragement, and Stewart returned to his Florida home refreshed and ready to start again.

The winning returned and when he won the Hertz Bay Hill classic in 1987 he handed over his winner's cheque for $108,000 to the Florida Hospital towards a cancer centre, to be named in honour of his father who died in 1985.

In his relatively short time in the game Payne Stewart has had to contend with major disappointments as well as the glories. He has a long career ahead of him and the

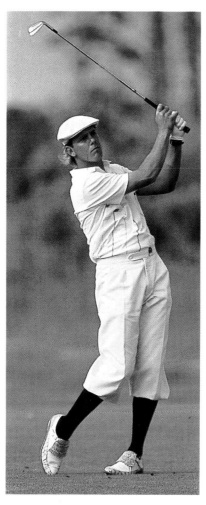

Above and left: Payne Stewart's best 'style' points are his dress as his shoes, his plus-fours and cap show . . .

> **'Payne Stewart has developed an infinite capacity for self destruction.'**
>
> *Ben Wright about Stewart's near-misses*

greatest testament to his ability came from none other than Lee Trevino when he said: 'He's a helluva player. He's long and he's aggressive. He has a lot of guts and works very hard on his game.'

Payne is distinguishable on the golf course by his brightly coloured plus-fours, socks, and his peaked cap; by far the most colourful dresser on the golf circuit. He obviously got his dress sense from his father because Bill, a successful furniture salesman, was well known locally for his brightly coloured sports jackets.

LEADING TOURNAMENT WINS

1982
Quad Cities Open

1983
Walt Disney Classic

1987
Hertz Bay Hill Classic

CURTIS STRANGE

Born: 20 January 1955, Norfolk, Virginia, USA	
Height: 5 ft 11 in (1.8 m)	
Weight: 168 lb (76.2 kg)	
Turned professional: 1976	
First US Tour win: 1979 Pensacola Open	

Curtis Strange opened the 1985 US Masters with an 80. In readiness for a quick getaway after missing the cut on day two he had his plane tickets in his bag but they soon became redundant. He played the next two rounds in 65 and 68 and the first nine of the final round in a four-under-par 32. He led the field by four shots at that stage, but then disaster struck. He three-putted at the 10th to drop his first shot of the day and at the 13th and 15th holes his iron-play became erratic and he found water. That was the end of what would have been the greatest comeback in golf: to win a modern-day major after opening with an 80. But it was not to be and Strange had to be content with a share of second place, two shots behind the German, Bernhard Langer.

The rest of the Curtis Strange story has, however, been one of triumph after triumph.

Record breaker
Records have followed Curtis's career. When he was tenth on the money-list in 1982 he amassed $263,378, the highest ever by a professional without registering a win. He was the top money-winner on the US Tour in 1985, and when he won the 1985 Canadian Open he took his winnings past the $½ million mark – the quickest that barrier had ever been broken in a season. His end-of-season total of $542,321 broke Tom Watson's five-year-old record by $12,000. In 1987 he confirmed himself the game's biggest money-winner in recent times when he topped the Tour money-list with an all-time

record $925,941, surpassing Greg Norman's old record of $653,296.

Golf in the family
Curtis Strange started playing golf at the age of seven and by the time he was eight was playing every day. His father was a professional golfer and owned the White Sands Country Club in Virginia Beach, Virginia. He was the inspiration behind Curtis's early days as a promising young golfer but, sadly, he died when Curtis was only 14.

> **'Winning breeds winning. Confidence breeds confidence. I guess that has something to do with the way I'm playing this year.'**
>
> *Summing up his great 1985 season*

Curtis Strange, the top US money winner in 1987 with $900,000-plus

Chandler Harper, a former professional and one of the game's foremost tutors, took the young aspirant under his wing and it was not long before Strange became the most outstanding amateur in Virginia. In 1975 he won the Eastern Amateur title which was an emotional win for Strange because his father won the same title in 1957. Shortly after winning the North and South Amateur in 1976 he turned professional and came through the Tour qualifying school in the spring of 1977.

Fearless, Strange never quits and is intent on saving every possible shot. That is what has made him the dedicated professional he is. Although he has never won a major tournament, he has dian Open, twice, and one of the four majors cannot be too far away for a man who keeps on breaking records.

HAL SUTTON

Born: 28 April 1958, Shreveport, Louisiana, USA	
Height: 6 ft 1 in (1.85 m)	
Weight: 185 lb (83.9 kg)	
Turned professional: 1981	
First US Tour win: 1982 Walt Disney World Golf Classic	

Hal Sutton burst on to the professional golfing scene in 1982 and set himself such high standards that few believed, or expected, him to maintain them. As Rookie of the Year in 1982 his earnings of $237,434 were the first over $200,000 for a Rookie. He went over that mark after beating Bill Britton with a birdie at the fourth extra hole to win the final event of the season, the Walt Disney Classic. Sutton followed his opening season in dramatic style by moving from eleventh on the money-list to first.

An outstanding second year

He had been the top money-winner for most of the 1983 season and edged out Fuzzy Zoeller by $9,000. A one-shot win over Bob Eastwood in the prestigious Tournament Players' Championship at Ponte Vedra netted him $126,000 alone and another $100,000 cheque came his way for fending off a challenge from Jack Nicklaus to win the US PGA Championship by one shot at the Riviera Club in Los Angeles.

Sutton took the PGA's Player of the Year title, but missed out on Ryder Cup selection. He has, however, made every team since then.

Early days

Hal took up the game as an 11-year-old when his father Howard, a wealthy oil man, was sent a set of clubs. His father didn't play golf and it was the young Hal who would often borrow them and sometimes play as many as 72 holes in a day. At college, however, Hal played most of the team sports and attracted the eye of the Arkansas American Football coach. But,

Hal Sutton compiled a most impressive record in his first five years as a professional

being a great competitor, Hal was often frustrated at playing on poor teams. He wanted to win all the time, but winning was out of his control in a team game. That is why he concentrated on golf.

He won the Louisiana State Junior title in 1974 and in 1980 he was the US Amateur Champion when he beat the former professional Bob Lewis, reinstated as amateur, by 8 & 7 at Pinehurst in North Carolina. Sutton was also on two US Walker Cup teams, in 1979 and 1981, and was the leading amateur in the 1981 Open at Royal St George's in Sandwich, Kent. Despite reaching the top of the amateur game he was undecided whether to turn professional and started working in his father's business. He eventually decided, because the love of golf was so strong, to give it a go at turning professional. He could, after all, go back to the family business if it didn't work out.

STYLE POINTS

Has a smooth graceful swing coupled with a delicate touch around the green.

'When I saw that 4-inch putt for a par at 18. I have a good percentage at handling 4-inch putts.'

When asked at what stage he thought he had won the 1983 PGA Championship

He came through the Tour school in the autumn of 1981 and his impact in the first two years was the Tour's gain and his father's business's loss.

Hal's talents were spotted by such notable agents as Mark McCormack and Vinnie Giles, who both wanted to sign him, but he went to an old friend, Fred Ridley, the 1975 US Amateur champion. Hal, his father, and Fred knew that his amateur successes and wealthy background would count for nothing on the Tour and life would be tougher than he'd ever known. But he soon became accepted for his talent and he enjoyed two great opening years.

Understandably he could not maintain the high standard of his first two years and was 26th on the money-list in 1984, but still with winnings of $227,949 – that is his lowest total in six years as a professional! By late 1987 his earnings had passed $2 million and he is among the top 20 money-winners of all-time.

*Left: Sutton eyes up a putt during the 1985 Ryder Cup at the Belfry
Below: Well, he's obviously hiding from somebody during the 1987 US Open at the Olympic Club!*

SAM TORRANCE

Born: 24 August 1953, Largs, Scotland
Height: 5 ft 11 in (1.8 m)
Weight: 189 lb (85.7 kg)
Turned professional: 1970
First European Tour win: 1976 Piccadilly Medal

In his 17-year career Sam Torrance has won nearly 20 top tournaments worldwide but none have given him as much pleasure as being the man who holed the winning putt to win the Ryder Cup for Europe at the Belfry course near Birmingham in 1985 after 28 years of American domination. With victory in sight for Europe Scot Torrance clinched it by beating his playing partner, US Open champion Andy North, at the last hole. Torrance hit a glorious drive while North went into the adjacent lake. Torrance knew he had won and secured the match, and he putted out for a birdie to make sure. As he walked up the fairway he could not hold back the emotional tears and those sentiments were shared by an entire nation and, somewhere in the large Belfry gallery, his father Bob.

> **'It was something you dream about. A magical moment I'll never forget as long as I live.'**
>
> *About his part in the Ryder Cup victory for Europe in 1985*

Debt to father

Sam owes a lot to his father who has coached him and encouraged him throughout his career and taught him everything he knows about golf. Bob, the professional at Largs Routenburg in Ayrshire, is a much respected teacher of the game and many of today's professionals go to him to have their problems solved.

Sam was a boy international at 17 and shortly afterwards turned professional. He became the assistant at Sunningdale in Berkshire to Arthur Lees, who carried on Sam's golfing education where dad had left off. Every year since 1978 he has finished in the top 20, reaching a personal best second place, behind Bernhard Langer, in 1984 thanks to three Tour wins. He has

Sam Torrance's greatest moment, with the 1985 Ryder Cup. It was his putt that clinched the match

topped £100,000 three times and in 1987 took his European career earnings past the £650,000-mark, the fifth best of all time.

Regarded as one of the Tour's most talented players, he really established himself in 1980 shortly after winning the Australian PGA title from a very strong field.

Winnings of £100,000 guaranteed him selection for the 1987 team and he won his first tournament for two years when he beat fellow 1985 Ryder Cup hero Jose Rivero to win the Italian Open.

Long before he became a national hero in the 1985 Ryder Cup, Sam Torrance was, to use snooker player Alex Higgins' phrase, 'the people's champion'. In recognition of his Ryder Cup exploits Sam was made a Freeman of the Cunninghame District of Ayrshire.

STYLE POINTS

Has a slow deliberate swing which has been described as the best in Europe. Also has a slow-motion putting action.

LEADING TOURNAMENT WINS

1976
Martini International

1980
Australian PGA

1981
Carrolls Irish Open

1982
Spanish Open
Portuguese Open

1983
Scandinavian Enterprise Open
Portuguese Open

1984
Tunisian Open
Benson & Hedges International
Sanyo Open

1985
Johnnie Walker Monte Carlo Open

1987
Italian Open

LEE TREVINO

Born: 1 December 1939, Dallas, Texas, USA
Height: 5 ft 11 in (1.7 m)
Weight: 180 lb (81.7 kg)
Turned professional: 1960
First US Tour win: 1968 US Open

In Lee Trevino golf possesses one of the great characters of modern-day sport. Constantly chatting and joking, that never detracts from the quality of his game as he constantly proves that golf can be fun.

> **'I swing the way I used to but when I look up the ball is going in a different direction!'**
>
> *Just before his 1984 PGA win*

Money to be made

Trevino realized he could make money out of golf when he was seven years old. He lived with his Mexican-born grandfather, and mother only 100 yards from the Dallas Athletic Club golf course in Texas. He regularly used to retrieve balls from the long rough alongside the seventh fairway. One day he received a dollar for five balls, and from that moment he realized there was money in the game.

When he was eight he first took an interest in the game from his position as caddie. Furthermore, the small amount of cash he brought home was a valuable contribution to the low family income. In addition to caddying, Trevino spent many long hours working hard on the family smallholding. He tells the tale that he was 20

> **'I can't wait to wake up in the morning, to hear what I have to say!'**

before he realized that Manual Labour wasn't a Mexican!

As soon as he picked up his first club Lee wanted to win. He is completely self taught, and that makes his subsequent list of achievements even greater. He left school at 14 and set his heart on doing nothing but play golf. He got a job at the local country club and at 15 entered his first tournament, the *Dallas Times Herald* tournament. He lost in the second round but that did not alter his appetite for the game. He served four years with the US Marines from 1956 but, because he played golf, he spent the last 18 months of his service in the Special Services, which allowed him to play a lot of golf.

Turning professional, but not serious

Lee turned professional after

One of the many great moments in the career of Lee Trevino: after winning the 1984 US PGA Championship at Shoal Creek

> **'I've stopped practising, I've stopped worrying, and I've got a new wife who travels with me. If I get any happier, I've got to be in heaven.'**
>
> *Shortly after his third marriage*

coming out of the Marines in 1960 but he did not join the Tour until 1967. His appearance alongside such men as Nicklaus, Palmer, Player and Snead had the pundits all asking if he could take the game seriously enough ever to be a great

Super Mex, Lee Trevino, in action during the 1985 Masters. Despite all his successes he has never won the Masters title

champion like them. He certainly had the ability, they wrote, but could he stop the clowning. Lee has, of course, proved them all wrong, and shown that clowning and serious golf can mix to produce a great player.

He totally astounded those pundits when he won his first Tour event the following year because that first win just happened to be the US Open. Furthermore he won with four rounds all under 70, the first time that had happened in the Open, and he beat Nicklaus by four shots. 'Supermex' as he became known, had arrived.

He added the Hawaiian Open that year and jumped from 45th to 6th in the money-list with earnings of $132,000. For once in their lives

> **'I always know which side a putt will break, it slopes towards the side of the green Herman is standing on.'**
>
> *Referring to his overweight caddie, Herman Mitchell*

the Trevino family no longer had to worry about money and Lee's first objective was to buy his mother and grandfather a new house, although they were reluctant to leave the family home.

Coming from poverty, Trevino knew all about hard times and after winning the Hawaiian Open he gave $10,000 of his earnings to the family of a friend who was tragically killed in a surfing accident.

Ups and downs in the 70s

In 1970 he topped the money-list

LEADING TOURNAMENT WINS

1968
US Open

1971
US Open
Canadian Open
British Open

1972
British Open

1974
World Series of Golf
US PGA Championship

1977
Canadian Open

1979
Canadian Open

1980
Tournament Players' Championship

1981
Tournament of Champions

1984
US PGA Championship

Left: Trevino, cold and unhappy during the 1985 Ryder Cup
Right: Lee Trevino again unhappy, this time behind some trees!

for the only time in his career, and was by then one of the most consistent golfers in the world.

The following year he enjoyed one of the best years of his career and, during one remarkable spell he completed one of golf's greatest achievements by winning the US and Canadian Opens and the Open in Britain, all within 23 days.

The British fans warmed to Trevino at Royal Birkdale in 1971 and thoroughly enjoyed his battle with the amiable Mr Lu from Taiwan. Those same British fans were to cheer another Trevino success at Muirfield in Scotland 12

months later when he holed two chips and a bunker shot to deprive Britain's Tony Jacklin of his second Open success.

In 1974 he won the first of his US PGA titles. In 1975 he was nearly killed by lightning at the Butler National Golf Club in Illinois during the Western Open. Trevino survived the ordeal but it was the start of a year long battle against a back complaint, which it was felt was brought on by the lightning. After an operation in November 1976 he soon showed signs that the old Trevino was on his way back.

He won two more Canadian Opens, the Tournament Players' Championship and the Tournament of Champions before possibly the greatest win of his career, the 1984 PGA Championship.

His greatest triumph, and a nice wedding present

Forty-four years of age at the time, he had not won on the US Tour for three and a half years and was still in pain with his back. But at Shoal Creek at Birmingham, Alabama, he overcame all handicaps to shoot four rounds in the 60s to outlast Gary Player and Lanny Wadkins.

His win took his career earnings over the $3 million mark, only the third man after Nicklaus and Watson to amass such a sum. It also made a nice wedding present for Lee and his third wife, Claudia, as they married earlier that year. Lee's first wife was Linda, whom he married in 1961; his second was also called Claudia, and their marriage lasted 20 years. Commenting after his marriage to Claudia (mark II), Lee said: 'That's handy, I won't have to change the towels in the bathroom . . .'

Trevino's great career was capped in 1985 when he was honoured with the non-playing captaincy of the US Ryder Cup team at the Belfry course near Birmingham. Sadly for Lee and the team, they suffered their first defeat since 1957.

Lee's influence on the game has been immense and despite not having a Tour win since 1984 he remains as popular as ever, whether it be on the golf course or behind the microphone where he gives expert summaries for American television.

Being self-taught it is hardly surprising that Trevino's swing is not exactly copy-book, but the arc of his swing is true and he has a perfect follow-through.

A record five Vardon trophies

The most wins of the Vardon Trophy, for the lowest stroke average on the US Tour, have been:

Wins		
5	Lee Trevino	1970-72, 1974, 1980
5	Billy Casper	1960, 1963, 1965-66, 1968
4	Sam Snead	1938, 1949-50, 1955
4	Arnold Palmer	1961-62, 1964, 1967

STYLE POINTS

A master of the fade. Can draw as well.

BOB TWAY

Born: 4 May 1959, Oklahoma City, Oklahoma, USA

Height: 6 ft 4 in (1.93 m)

Weight: 180 lb (81.7 kg)

Turned professional: 1981

First professional win: 1986 Shearson Lehman Bros–Andy Williams Open

An excellent striker of the ball with a swing modelled on Tom Weiskopf's, Bob Tway has emerged as one of the best prospects to hit the US professional ranks in the 1980s. In addition to his ideal swing, in which he prefers to play from right to left, he has perfected his putting stroke, a feature of his game he neglected while getting his swing right.

Golfing in the family

Golf has always run in the Tway family as his father and grandfather were keen players. The family moved house frequently when Bob was a youngster, but one priority was always that each new house should be near a golf course. Bob's father, Robert, is a member of the Board of the Georgia Golf Association and brother Scott

Left: The chip at the 18th that won Bob Tway the 1986 US PGA Championship from Greg Norman

Opposite page: Tway proudly holds aloft the large US PGA trophy after his success at Inverness

played college golf at Georgia Southern. Tway picked up his first club when he was five, when he used to follow his father and grandfather around the course. He entered his first junior tournament at the age of seven.

Because of his height, Bob also played basketball during his first two years at high school but that never overtook his interest in, and love of, golf. At college he became an outstanding golfer and was named the 1981 Fred Haskins Trophy winner as the outstanding college player of the year. Under the guidance of Mike Holder, the golf coach at Oklahoma State University, Tway's game matured beyond his years. Bob still goes back to Holder, known to him as 'coach', for advice and guidance.

A pretty fiery competitor at one time, Bob Tway's bad temper was cured during his high school days. During a match he threw his putter up in the air after making a bad shot. It landed in a tree and when it eventually confirmed Newton's law of gravity, it hit the ground minus its head and he had to putt out with a number 8 iron for the remainder of the tournament.

Tway turned professional in 1981 but struggled to get through the PGA qualifying school. He made it at the third attempt. While waiting to get on the US Tour he played the Asian and European Tours, but with little success.

A memorable rookie

Once he got through the qualifying school he played very few tournaments in the first half of the 1985 season because of his low qualifying position. Midway through the season, however, he was in contention for his first title, the St Jude Memphis Classic but had to be content with fourth place after opening rounds of 69–69. His best

result of his Rookie season came less than a month later when he finished second to Dan Forsman in the Mile High Life tournament at Illinois. He ended the season by finishing third in the Seiko-Tucson Match-Play Championship and collected the then biggest cheque of his career, $60,000.

Bob Tway was delighted with his Rookie season, 1985, during which he won $164,023 and finished 45th on the money-list. But he must surely never have imagined what the following season had in store for him: he won four

Unorthodox stance with his hands very low and his back hunched.

US Tour tournaments, culminating in the US PGA championship at Inverness in Ohio and was second in the money-list with a massive $652,780. He was also named the US PGA's Player of the Year.

Even more memorable second year
He beat Bernhard Langer in a

play-off to win his first tournament, the Shearson Lehman Bros–Andy Williams Open. By the time the US PGA Championship came around, Tway and Australian Greg Norman were heading the US money-list and it was the same pair who were to take centre stage in the last major of the season.

Norman led going into the final

round, just as he had done in every major during the season. Tway cut Norman's big lead to four strokes on the third day after a blistering course record 64. Because of appalling weather the final day's play was suspended after the two leaders had played only two holes, and play was put back a day. The delay seemed to be to Tway's advantage.

As they teed off at the 18th, the players were level. With their second shots Tway found a bunker while Norman hit the green before rolling into some thick rough.

Tway chipped into the hole from the sand, Norman made a bogey and Tway crowned a memorable second season with this first major.

The man who plays such calculated golf with a level temperament that is the envy of many of his fellow professionals, eventually showed his true emotions after his win. Tway rarely shows much emotion, hence his collection of nicknames: Poker Face, the Tin Man and the Ice Man. But after taking the PGA title he broke down in a flood of tears in front of millions of watching TV fans. Despite the efforts of wife Tammie to wipe them away they still kept coming and for the first time, the *real* Bob Tway was seen.

Third year unlucky?

His third season was nowhere as memorable as his second. He slipped more than 40 places down the money-list and missed out on a place in the 1987 US Ryder Cup team. But after the euphoria of that great 1986 season, the man hailed as the next superstar of American golf should soon be back on the winning trail.

The next superstar?

Two of the game's greats, Lee Trevino and Gary Player have both hailed Tway as a new star. The South African spotted his potential when playing a tournament with him in 1983, while Trevino made the prediction after watching him in action during the 1986 US Open. In the same competition the eventual winner, Ray Floyd, said Tway was by far the best putter he had ever seen.

With men like that predicting your future then Bob Tway must feel confident of coming back and emulating his magical year of 1986.

LEADING TOURNAMENT WINS

1986
Shearson Lehman Bros–Andy Williams Open
Manufacturers Hanover–Westchester Classic
Georgia Pacific Atlanta Classic
US PGA Championship

Bob Tway certainly took the US golfing scene by storm in 1986. In addition to winning his first major he was second to Greg Norman on the money-list and won four events

LANNY WADKINS

Born:	5 December 1949, Richmond, Virginia, USA
Height:	5 ft 9 in (1.75 m)
Weight:	160 lb (72.6 kg)
Turned professional:	1971
First US Tour win:	1972 Sahara Invitational

Although Lanny Wadkins has won more than 15 events including the US PGA Championship and some of the most prestigious events on the US Tour, the greatest thrill he has had from the sport was in being named the 1985 PGA Player of the Year, an accolade previously bestowed on such greats as Ben Hogan, Sam Snead, Arnold Palmer and Jack Nicklaus.

Wadkins won the honour by winning three times during the season and finishing second in the money-list to Curtis Strange with earnings of $446,893.

'Put a pin in the middle of a lake and Lanny will attack it.'

John Mahaffey on Lanny's attacking game

A member of the $3 million club

Since coming through the Tour school in the autumn of 1971 Wadkins has joined the small band of players who have made $3 million during their careers. Since 1981 his lowest seasonal total has been $198,000.

An outstanding amateur

Lanny started playing golf at the age of eight with younger brother Bobby, who is also a current professional. They played at the Meadowbrook Golf Club at Richmond under the watchful eye of the resident professional, J. G. Lumpkin. Lanny was outstanding as an amateur and started his great career in 1963 by winning the National Pee Wee title. He followed that with victories in the Southern, Eastern and Western Amateur championships and in 1970 he was the US Amateur champion when his total of 279 beat fellow professional Tom Kite by one stroke. In the eight years the championship was contested over stroke-play Wadkins' score was the lowest winning total.

Before turning professional Wadkins had also won himself international honours as a member of the victorious US team in the World Amateur Team championship and as a member of the 1969 and 1971 US Walker Cup teams.

Ups and downs

In his Rookie year as a professional, 1972, Lanny was tenth on the money-list with winnings of $116,616. The following year, thanks to wins in the Byron Nelson Classic and USI Classic, he was

One of the game's most popular guys, Lanny Wadkins. Younger brother Bobby is also a professional but Lanny has the better record on the US Tour

fifth with winnings of more than $200,000.

There was a decline in his game for several years and he missed a large part of the 1975 season after an operation. In 1977, however, victory in his one and only major elevated him to third in the money-list.

In winning his first major, the US PGA Championship at Pebble Beach in California, he had to display great calmness in hauling back both Gene Littler and Jack Nicklaus before forcing a play-off with the 47-year-old Littler. In the first sudden-death to decide a major championship Lanny had to hole a 20-footer (6 metres) at the first extra hole to stay alive and two holes later he clinched the championship with a four to Littler's five.

Apart from a barren spell between 1979 and 1982 Wadkins has been a regular Tour winner since

Wadkins won the 1977 US PGA Championship; ten years later he had a great chance to win the title again but lost a play-off to Larry Nelson

then and in 1987 was involved in another exciting play-off for the US PGA Championship, ten years after his epic encounter with Littler.

This time the venue was the PGA National at Palm Beach Gardens in Florida. As the players approached the 72nd hole any one of half a dozen men could have won the title but one by one they fell by the wayside. Larry Nelson was in the clubhouse with a 287 and Wadkins had a 6-foot (1.8 metre) putt to force the play-off. He made it, but at the first extra hole he missed from 4 feet (1.22 metres) after Nelson had sunk a 6-footer (1.8 metres) for his par, and the title.

Despite that disappointment Wadkins was among the leaders on the money-list with more than $500,000 and he gained a US Ryder Cup place, his fifth selection. When the Cup had last been played on US soil, at the PGA National in 1983, it was Lanny's half against Jose Maria Canizares which had set up the home team's narrow one-point win. Although he beat Ken Brown in 1987, however, victory had already gone to the Europeans.

Lanny Wadkins is one of the toughest competitors on the US Tour. He attacks everything and gets a big kick out of playing that way. Despite his bold approach he never takes chances if the risk is high.

LEADING TOURNAMENT WINS

1977
*US PGA Championship
World Series of Golf*

1979
Tournament Players' Championship

1982
Tournament of Champions

1983
Tournament of Champions

TOM WATSON

Born: 4 September 1949, Kansas City, Missouri, USA	
Height: 5 ft 9 in (1.75 m)	
Weight: 161 lb (73 kg)	
Turned professional: 1971	
First US Tour win: 1974 Western Open	

With the arrival of Tom Watson in the mid-1970s there came another young pretender to Jack Nicklaus' crown. But this time the challenge did not fade as with all previous aspirants, and Watson remained to claim legitimately to be Nicklaus' successor.

A youthful start

A psychology graduate from Stanford University, Tom was introduced to golf by his scratch-handicap father when only six. He was a four-time winner of the Missouri State Amateur title and turned professional in 1971, collecting $1,065 from his first Tour event, the Kaiser International. Taught to play the game by Stan Thirsk, Tom Watson has risen to become one of the game's greatest players.

> **'My golf swing is like ironing a shirt. You get one side smoothed out, turn it over and there is a big wrinkle on the other side. You then iron that side, turn it over and there's another wrinkle.'**
>
> *On the problems he had with his swing in 1987*

Take-off in the mid-70s

The first of his 32 Tour wins, which put him in ninth place of all time for most wins on the US Tour, was the 1974 Western Open. The following year he won the first of his post-war record-equalling five British Opens when he beat the unfortunate Australian Jack Newton in a play-off at Carnoustie in Scotland. Surprisingly Tom went without a win in 1976 but then started his dominance of US golf that was to last for nearly a decade.

Four Tour wins in 1977, including the US Masters, put him at the top of the money-list for the first of four consecutive years. Winning the Masters gave him great personal satisfaction because he beat

> **'Galleries understand the game and are very respectful. In my opinion, it's the last civilized country left in the world.'**
>
> *About the British fans after capturing his fifth British Open title in 1983*

Nicklaus in a head-to-head contest over the last three rounds to confirm his arrival as the Golden Bear's successor. Winning was particularly joyful after disappointment: he had been in with a chance of winning the 1974 and 1975 US Opens but lost both in the final round. Also, the two tournaments before the Masters had been taken away from Tom in the last round.

He also beat Nicklaus in a record-breaking scoring spree at Turnberry in Ayrshire to win his second British Open in 1977.

Between 1978 and 1980 Watson won 16 more Tour events, including the Tournament of Champions in 1979, but added only one more

Watson in action during the 1987 US Open. He showed signs of his old magic by finishing second to Scott Simpson

The leading British Open winners

Wins
6	Harry Vardon (GB)	1896, 1898-99, 1903, 1911, 1914
5	James Braid (GB)	1901, 1905-06, 1908, 1910
5	J. H. Taylor (GB)	1894-95, 1900, 1909, 1913
5	Peter Thomson (Aus)	1954-56, 1958, 1965
5	Tom Watson (USA)	1975, 1977, 1980, 1982-83

LEADING TOURNAMENT WINS

1975
British Open
World Series of Golf

1977
US Masters
British Open

1980
British Open

1981
US Masters

1982
US Open
British Open

1983
British Open

major when he beat Lee Trevino by four shots to win the 1980 Open at Muirfield in Scotland. He remained the top money-winner and in 1980 was the first man to pass the $500,000 mark for a season.

Watson lost his number one position to Tom Kite in 1981 but

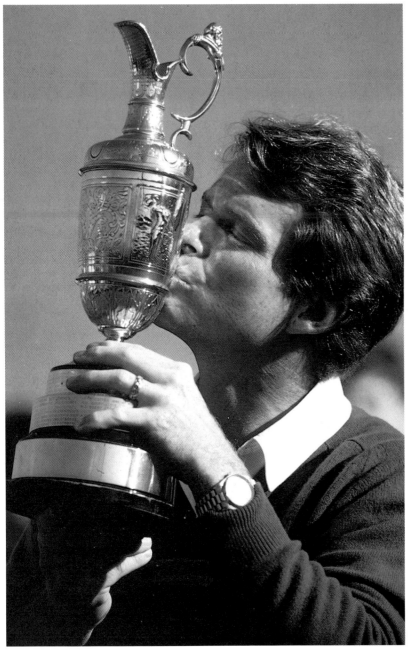

won his second US Masters title and two other Tour events, the New Orleans Open and Atlanta Classic.

In 1982 he won the US Open with one of golf's most memorable shots. It was at Pebble Beach in California. His two-iron off the tee at the par-three 17th found heavy rough on the side of the green. He was level with Nicklaus who had finished his round. Tom was looking for a par to stay level, but realistically a bogey was on the cards. He played the perfect pitch, it went in the hole for another birdie and a birdie at the last ensured Tom his first US Open by two shots.

Watson also won his fourth Open in Britain in 1982 when he beat Briton Peter Oosterhuis and South African Nick Price by one shot at Troon in Scotland.

In 1987 Watson won the Nabisco Challenge and finished the season fifth on the money list with $616,351

American failure, European success

Tom slumped to his lowest position on the money list for ten years in 1983 when he was twelfth and for the first time since 1976 he failed to win on the US Tour. He continued winning elsewhere, including equalling Peter Thomson's post-war record of five Open wins in Britain when he beat Hale Irwin and Andy Bean to win by one stroke at the Royal Birkdale course in Merseyside, his only Open success in England.

Despite talk of deterioration in Watson's game he came back in 1984 to win the Seiko-Tucson Match-Play, Tournament of Champions and Western Open to top the money-list for the fifth time in his career and win the PGA Player of the Year award for the sixth time.

He had been without a win since 1984 but came back in 1987 to win the Nabisco Challenge. He finished fifth on the money-list with a personal best $616,351 and took his career earnings to $4,700,000, just $275,000 behind Nicklaus.

Watson is respected by golf administrators, his fellow professionals and golf fans the world over, particularly in Britain. He has been a model professional and served his country as a member of the Ryder Cup team in 1977, 1981 and 1983. Despite problems with his swing in 1987 he served notice that he is still a force to be reckoned with in the majors as his second to Scott Simpson in the US Open, and seventh in the British Open showed.

Married and with two children, Tom and wife Linda have been childhood sweethearts. They first met when Tom was 13 and they were both performing in Gilbert and Sullivan's *Pirates of Penzance* during their school days.

Tom Watson after winning his third British Open, at Muirfield in 1980

STYLE POINTS

Makes good use of his knees when playing chip shots.

KATHY WHITWORTH

Born: 27 September 1939, Monahans, Texas, USA

Height: 5 ft 9 in (1.75 m)

Weight: 151 lb (68.5 kg)

Turned professional: 1958

First US LPGA Tour win: 1962 Kelly Girl Open

Kathy Whitworth is the equivalent in women's golf of Sam Snead in the men's game. She has won a record 88 US LPGA events, which is four more than Snead, and like her great male counterpart, has inexplicably never won the US Open. Sam came close on several occasions but the nearest Kathy came was in 1971 when she finished second to JoAnne Carner, but was seven shots adrift.

Despite her failure to win the Open she has been the greatest woman golfer of modern times, and took over the mantle when Mickey Wright curtailed her playing days in the mid-1960s.

The greatest female golfer of all time

Kathy started playing golf at 15 and three years later turned professional. Between 1965 and 1973 she was the top money-winner a record eight times in nine years and during that spell won 61 of her unequalled 88 tournaments. She spent a few years in the wilderness between 1974 and 1980 and, at that time was still behind Mickey Wright's record of 82 US Tour wins. Kathy was determined to better that total and in the 1982 Lady Michelob Tournament she succeeded. A year earlier she had become the first female golfer to win $1 million in a career when finishing third in the Open.

Kathy Whitworth has been all that is good in women's golf. She was inducted into the Hall of Fame in 1975 and served as a Player Director of the US LPGA in 1986 and 1987. She is also an active member of the American President's Campaign Council Against Drug Abuse.

Since her heady return to her rightful place amongst the top women golfers in the early 1980s, Kathy has steadily slipped down the rankings and has not won on Tour since the 1985 United Virginia Bank Classic but, even at 48, Kathy Whitworth is too good to be ignored. She is still capable of winning and if she can return from the wilderness once, she can do it a second time.

The greatest ever winner in women's golf – Kathy Whitworth. She has won 88 US LPGA events, a figure that is four more than Sam Snead's male record

LEADING TOURNAMENT WINS

1965
Titleholders' Championship

1966
Titleholders' Championship

1967
US LPGA Championship
Western Open

1971
US LPGA Championship

1975
US LPGA Championship

1982
US LPGA Championship

STYLE POINTS

Has a flat swing but safely sends the ball down the middle. One of the best female players on the putting surface.

IAN WOOSNAM

Born: 2 March 1958, St Martins, Shropshire, England

Height: 5 ft 4½ in (1.64 m)

Weight: 147 lb (66.7 kg)

Turned professional: 1976

First European Tour win: 1982 Swiss Open

The Shropshire-based Welshman Ian Woosnam is probably the biggest hitter on the European circuit, and pound-for-pound is one of the strongest players on the Tour.

Ever since he won his first European tournament in 1982 Woosnam has been regarded as one of the best prospects to emerge from Britain in the 1980s and his successful 1987 season bore those predictions out. He was the top European money-winner with more than £250,000 and won five tournaments, the Jersey, Madrid and Scottish Opens, the Lancôme Trophy and Suntory Match-play Championship. He then helped Wales to win the World Cup and Ian won the individual title. He ended the season with victory in the Sun City Million.

What a year 1987 was for Ian Woosnam – he could hardly go wrong. Winning the Ryder Cup in America was one of many highlights

Ryder Cup glory

Finishing top of the Order of Merit assured Ian inclusion in Tony Jacklin's Ryder Cup team, his third successive selection and he was one of Europe's inspirations in the first-ever victory on American soil.

'No, I want to be No. 1.'

When asked if he was happy with retaining his top ten position for the third successive year in 1984

In 1986 at the Belfry course near Birmingham Woosnam enjoyed one of the best wins of his career, the Lawrence Batley Tournament Player's Championship. Despite having a bad opening three rounds, in which his putting let him down, as it had so often in the past, he suddenly had a flash of inspiration and decided to switch to a method of putting he had been experimenting with in practice.

He started lining the putter up square to the hole from behind, and then moved round to take up his address without changing anything. Suddenly it worked. He had been aiming right and missing, but now the putts went in and he won

---

'Perhaps if I dyed my hair peroxide blonde and called myself the Great White Tadpole that would help.'

His suggestion for overcoming his comparative obscurity after beating a quality field to win the 1987 Madrid Open

---

the tournament with an 11-under-par 277 to become the first Briton to win in eight major stroke-play championships held over the famous course.

An unwanted European 'record'

Although he finished fourth on the Order of Merit in 1986 it was not all success for Woosnam. In the French Open at La Bouille he took 16 at the par-three third hole in his round of 81, to create a new European PGA record which he would be glad to lose.

Woosnam did little as an amateur and it was a surprise when he turned professional at 18.

Ian developed his strong arms driving a tractor and doing manual work around the family farm on which he was brought up. Although born in England, by three miles, he proudly claims to be

'a Taff to the core'. Both his parents are Welsh and Ian learnt his golf on the Llanmynech course which has 15 holes in Wales and three in England! It is therefore hardly surprising that he rates his win in the 1983 Silk Cut Masters as one of the most pleasing of his career: it was at St Pierre, Chepstow – on Welsh soil.

Left: Ian Woosnam is now one of Britain's best golfers. Can he repeat his successes in 1988?

Right: A young 'caddie' is helping Ian Woosnam to celebrate his victory in the Suntory World Match-Play Championship

FUZZY ZOELLER

Born:	11 November 1951, New Albany, Indiana, USA
Height:	5 ft 10 in (1.78 m)
Weight:	190 lb (86.2 kg)
Turned professional:	1973
First US Tour win:	1979 Wickes Andy Williams–San Diego Open

Frank Urban Zoeller, known as Fuzzy because of his initials owes his success in world golf to his attitude and belief that golf is *only* a game and nothing more. He has a simple philosophy: 'Hit it. Find it. Hit it again, add'em up and see what you've got!' . . .

'I'd done something I'd been fantasizing about since I was 10.'

After winning the 1979 US Masters

An infant golfer

Fuzzy has been swinging a golf club since he was three and entered his first tournament at the age of five. He also loved playing baseball and his father, fed up with taking him from golf to baseball, and vice versa, made him choose when he was eight which one he wanted. He chose golf.

Golf was his first love at college but he also played basketball in the winter when golf wasn't possible in his home town. It was while playing basketball that his now renowned back trouble started when somebody landed on him during a match.

Constant back pains have plagued him throughout his career. Just before the start of the 1984 US PGA at Shoal Creek in Alabama he collapsed after getting a severe spasm in his back after bending down and had to miss the tournament. Ironically it was won by another of the game's back-sufferers, Lee Trevino.

After a year at Houston University he dropped out because his coach accused him of being 'crazy'.

Fuzzy, being a great sportsman, used to applaud or congratulate opponents for making a good shot. His coach would tell him off for such an action, saying it helped the opponent to relax. That was a line of thinking Fuzzy did not understand, and still doesn't today.

Fuzzy has been on the US Tour since 1975 and first attracted attention in 1976 when he equalled a Tour record with eight consecutive birdies in the Quad Cities Open.

A sensational first major

He hit the headlines in 1979 when he won his first event, the San

Fuzzy Zoeller in action after his back troubles had cleared up

Diego Open and then in the same year became the first man since Horton Smith in 1934, and Gene Sarzen the following year, to win at the first attempt.

He trailed Ed Sneed by six shots going into the final round and was sitting in the players' tent on 280, along with Tom Watson. They were expecting a share of second place but Sneed bogeyed the last hole and created a play-off. Fuzzy won at the second extra hole.

Since then Zoeller's ten Tour wins have helped take his career earnings past $2 million. He became the 18th player to reach that landmark in 1987. Even during his painful year of 1984 Zoeller still managed to win $157,000.

More than $90,000 of that was as a result of winning his second major, the US Open at Winged Foot in New York. His win, however, was nearly a reversal of his 1979 US Masters triumph. He led Greg Norman by three shots with five to play when at the 18th Norman holed a 40-footer (12-metres) to force the play-off. Unlike Sneed's demise at Augusta five years earlier, Zoeller came back in fine style to win the 18-hole play off by an impressive eight shots.

Zoeller was back in business in 1985 after an operation on his back and he won the Hertz Bay Hill Classic. All signs that his troubles were over were evident in 1986 when he won three tournaments and $358,000 in prize money.

Winless in 1987 he was still among the top 50 and continued to provide entertainment for the galleries and fellow professionals, all of whom are glad to see that the injury which so nearly ended his career has been put right.

Shortly before Zoeller's problems; winning the 1984 US Open at Winged Foot, his first major success since winning the Masters at the first attempt in 1979

POST-1945 WINNERS OF MAJOR CHAMPIONSHIPS

(The players whose names appear in italics are those appearing in the Who's Who)

BRITISH OPEN

Year	Winner	Score	Venue	Year	Winner	Score	Venue	Year	Winner	Score	Venue
1946	Sam Snead	290	St Andrews	1960	Kel Nagle	278	St Andrews	1974	*Gary Player*	282	Royal Lytham
1947	Fred Daly	293	Hoylake	1961	*Arnold Palmer*	284	Royal Birkdale	1975	*Tom Watson*	279	Carnoustie
1948	Henry Cotton	284	Muirfield	1962	*Arnold Palmer*	276	Troon	1976	*Johnny Miller*	279	Royal Birkdale
1949	Bobby Locke	283	Sandwich	1963	Bob Charles	277	Royal Lytham	1977	*Tom Watson*	268	Turnberry
1950	Bobby Locke	279	Troon	1964	Tony Lema	279	St Andrews	1978	*Jack Nicklaus*	281	St Andrews
1951	Max Faulkner	285	Portrush	1965	Peter Thomson	285	Royal Birkdale	1979	*S. Ballesteros*	283	Royal Lytham
1952	Bobby Locke	287	Royal Lytham	1966	*Jack Nicklaus*	282	Muirfield	1980	*Tom Watson*	271	Muirfield
1953	Ben Hogan	282	Carnoustie	1967	R.de Vicenzo	278	Hoylake	1981	Bill Rogers	276	Sandwich
1954	Peter Thomson	283	Royal Birkdale	1968	*Gary Player*	289	Carnoustie	1982	*Tom Watson*	284	Royal Troon
1955	Peter Thomson	281	St Andrews	1969	*Tony Jacklin*	280	Royal Lytham	1983	*Tom Watson*	275	Royal Birkdale
1956	Peter Thomson	286	Hoylake	1970	*Jack Nicklaus*	283	St Andrews	1984	*S. Ballesteros*	276	St Andrews
1957	Bobby Locke	279	St Andrews	1971	*Lee Trevino*	278	Royal Birkdale	1985	*Sandy Lyle*	282	Sandwich
1958	Peter Thomson	278	Royal Lytham	1972	*Lee Trevino*	278	Muirfield	1986	*Greg Norman*	280	Turnberry
1959	*Gary Player*	284	Muirfield	1973	Tom Weiskopf	276	Troon	1987	*Nick Faldo*	279	Muirfield

UNITED STATES OPEN

Year	Winner	Score	Venue	Year	Winner	Score	Venue	Year	Winner	Score	Venue
1946	Lloyd Mangrum	284	Canterbury	1960	*Arnold Palmer*	280	Cherry Hills	1974	*Hale Irwin*	287	Winged Foot
1947	Lew Worsham	282	St Louis	1961	Gene Littler	281	Oakland Hills	1975	Lou Graham	287	Medinah
1948	Ben Hogan	276	Riviera	1962	*Jack Nicklaus*	283	Oakmont	1976	*Jerry Pate*	277	Atlanta
1949	Cary Middlecoff	286	Medinah	1963	Julius Boros	293	Brookline	1977	*Hubert Green*	278	Southern Hills
1950	Ben Hogan	287	Merion	1964	Ken Venturi	278	Congressional	1978	Andy North	285	Cherry Hills
1951	Ben Hogan	287	Oakland Hills	1965	*Gary Player*	282	Bellerive	1979	*Hale Irwin*	284	Inverness
1952	Julius Boros	281	Northwood	1966	Billy Casper	278	Olympic	1980	*Jack Nicklaus*	272	Baltusrol
1953	Ben Hogan	283	Oakmont	1967	*Jack Nicklaus*	275	Baltusrol	1981	*David Graham*	273	Merion
1954	Ed Furgol	284	Baltusrol	1968	*Lee Trevino*	275	Oak Hill	1982	*Tom Watson*	282	Pebble Beach
1955	Jack Fleck	287	Olympic	1969	Orville Moody	281	Champions	1983	*Larry Nelson*	280	Oakmont
1956	Cary Middlecoff	281	Oak Hill	1970	*Tony Jacklin*	281	Hazeltine	1984	*Fuzzy Zoeller*	276	Winged Foot
1957	Dick Mayer	282	Inverness	1971	*Lee Trevino*	280	Merion	1985	Andy North	279	Oakland Hills
1958	Tommy Bolt	283	Southern Hills	1972	*Jack Nicklaus*	290	Pebble Beach	1986	*Ray Floyd*	279	Shinnecock H.
1959	Billy Casper	282	Winged Foot	1973	*Johnny Miller*	279	Oakmont	1987	*Scott Simpson*	277	Olympic Club

UNITED STATES PGA CHAMPIONSHIP

Year	Winner	Score	Venue	Year	Winner	Score	Venue	Year	Winner	Score	Venue
1946	Ben Hogan	6 & 4	Portland	1960	Jay Hebert	281	Firestone	1974	*Lee Trevino*	276	Tanglewood
1947	Jim Ferrier	2 & 1	Plum Hollow	1961	Jerry Barber	277	Olympia Flds	1975	*Jack Nicklaus*	276	Firestone
1948	Ben Hogan	7 & 6	Norwood Hills	1962	*Gary Player*	278	Aronomink	1976	Dave Stockton	281	Congressional
1949	Sam Snead	3 & 2	Hermitage	1963	*Jack Nicklaus*	279	Dallas	1977	*Lanny Wadkins*	282	Pebble Beach
1950	Chandler Harper	4 & 3	Scioto	1964	Bobby Nichols	271	Columbus	1978	*John Mahaffey*	276	Oakmont
1951	Sam Snead	7 & 6	Oakmont	1965	Dave Marr	280	Laurel Valley	1979	*David Graham*	272	Oakland Hills
1952	Jim Turnesa	1 up	Big Spring	1966	Al Geiberger	280	Firestone	1980	*Jack Nicklaus*	274	Oak Hill
1953	Walter Burkemo	2 & 1	Birmingham	1967	Don January	281	Columbine	1981	*Larry Nelson*	273	Atlanta
1954	Chick Harbert	4 & 3	Keller	1968	Julius Boros	281	Pecan Valley	1982	*Ray Floyd*	272	Southern Hills
1955	Doug Ford	4 & 3	Meadowbrook	1969	*Ray Floyd*	276	NCR, Dayton	1983	*Hal Sutton*	274	Riviera
1956	Jack Burke	3 & 2	Blue Hill	1970	Dave Stockton	279	Southern Hills	1984	*Lee Trevino*	273	Shoal Creek
1957	Lionel Hebert	2 & 1	Miami Valley	1971	*Jack Nicklaus*	281	PGA National	1985	*Hubert Green*	278	Cherry Hills
1958	Dow Finsterwald	276	Llanerch	1972	*Gary Player*	281	Oakland Hills	1986	*Bob Tway*	276	Toledo
1959	Bob Rosburg	277	Minneapolis	1973	*Jack Nicklaus*	277	Canterbury	1987	*Larry Nelson*	287	PGA National

US MASTERS (All played at Augusta, Georgia)

Year	Winner	Score	Year	Winner	Score	Year	Winner	Score	Year	Winner	Score
1946	Herman Keiser	282	1957	Doug Ford	282	1968	Bob Goalby	277	1979	*Fuzzy Zoeller*	280
1947	Jimmy Demaret	281	1958	*Arnold Palmer*	284	1969	George Archer	281	1980	*Severiano Ballesteros*	275
1948	Claude Harmon	279	1959	Art Wall, Jnr	284	1970	Billy Casper	279	1981	*Tom Watson*	280
1949	Sam Snead	282	1960	*Arnold Palmer*	282	1971	Charles Coody	279	1982	*Craig Stadler*	284
1950	Jimmy Demaret	283	1961	*Gary Player*	280	1972	*Jack Nicklaus*	286	1983	*Severiano Ballesteros*	280
1951	Ben Hogan	280	1962	*Arnold Palmer*	280	1973	Tommy Aaron	283	1984	*Ben Crenshaw*	277
1952	Sam Snead	286	1963	*Jack Nicklaus*	286	1974	*Gary Player*	278	1985	*Bernhard Langer*	282
1953	Ben Hogan	274	1964	*Arnold Palmer*	276	1975	*Jack Nicklaus*	276	1986	*Jack Nicklaus*	279
1954	Sam Snead	289	1965	*Jack Nicklaus*	271	1976	*Ray Floyd*	271	1987	*Larry Mize*	285
1955	Cary Middlecoff	279	1966	*Jack Nicklaus*	288	1977	*Tom Watson*	276			
1956	Jack Burke, Jnr	289	1967	Gay Brewer	280	1978	*Gary Player*	277			